ED

ARKANSAS

ARKANSAS BY ROAD

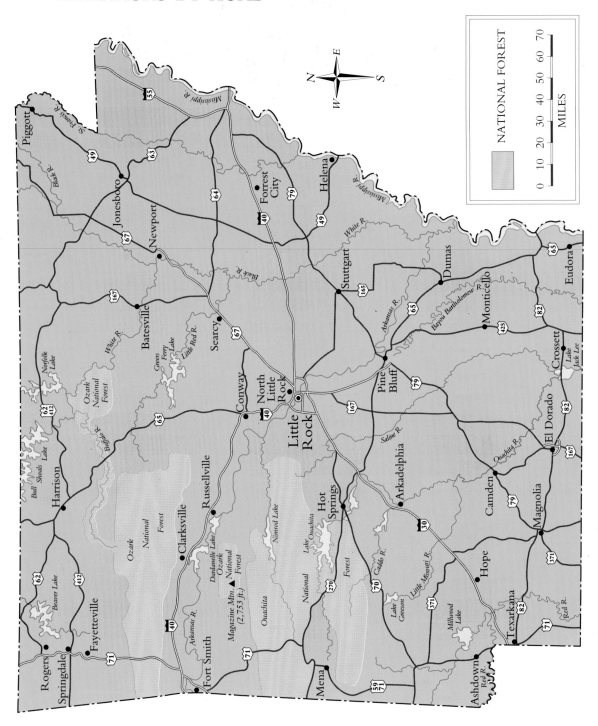

CELEBRATE THE STATES
ARKANSAS

Linda Jacobs Altman

BENCHMARK BOOKS

MARSHALL CAVENDISH
NEW YORK

Benchmark Books
Marshall Cavendish Corporation
99 White Plains Road
Tarrytown, New York 10591-9001

Library of Congress Cataloging-in-Publication Data
Altman, Linda Jacobs, date
Arkansas / Linda Altman.
p.   cm.—(Celebrate the states)
Includes bibliographical references (p.) and index.
Summary: Discusses the geographic features, history, government, people,
and attractions of the state known as the Natural State.
ISBN 0-7614-0672-7 (lib. bdg.)
1. Arkansas—Juvenile literature. [1. Arkansas.] I. Title. II. Series.
F411.3.A48   2000   976.7—dc21   98-43959   CIP   AC

Maps and graphics supplied by Oxford Cartographers, Oxford, England

Photo research by Candlepants Incorporated

Cover photo: Matt Bradley

The photographs in this book are used by permission and through the courtesy of: *Matt Bradley*: 6-7, 15, 17,
21, 22, 58, 62(top & bottom), 63(top & bottom), 66, 68, 70-71, 75, 79, 81, 84, 87, 88-89, 104-105, 110-
111, 115, 116, back cover. *Ozark Yesteryear Photography*: Tom Coker, 10- 11, 73, 110(top). *Photo Researchers,
Inc.*: Bruce Roberts, 14; Garry D. McMichael, 19, 114; Dr. Paul A. Zahl, 23; Gregory K. Scott, 25(top); Ray
Coleman, 25(bottom); Chromosohm/Sohm, 50-51; Mike Jackson, 60; Andy Levin, 80; M.H. Sharp, 119(top);
H.S. Banton, 119(bottom); Steve Coombs, 122; Junebug Clark, 124. *Arkansas Department of Parks and
Tourism*: A.C. Haralson, 27, 61, 64, 108, 126, 137; Gary Don, 78; Craig Ogilvie. *Painting by
WilliamMcNamara, 28-29. From nouveaux voyages dans l'Amerique septentrionale (Amsterdam [i.e. Paris] 1777),
31. The Museum of Mobile: 33. Arkansas History Commission: 34, 39, 43, 45. UALR Archives and Special
Collections, photo 59.42 Drilling crew spudding in the Bradstreet Laney No. 2 in the Smackover fields: 44. Corbis*:
Bettmann, 46, 54, 99, 128, 129(right), 130, 132(top), 133(top & bottom); Joseph Sohm/ChromoSohm Inc.,
102. *Archive Photos*: Win McNamee/Reuters, 48; Sue Ogrocki/Reuters, 91; Popperfoto, 93; Consolidated
News, 94, 97; Jeff Mitchell/Reuters, 101; Frank Capri/SAGA, 129 (left); Sporting News, 131; Fotos
International, 132(bottom); Frank Driggs Collection, 134, 135. *Image Bank*: Adrien Duey, 76.

Printed in Italy

3   5   6   4

CONTENTS

INTRODUCTION   ARKANSAS IS . . .   6

1 GEOGRAPHY   A GOOD AND PLEASANT LAND   10
LANDFORMS • THE CLIMATE • WATERWAYS • PLANTS AND ANIMALS •
PROTECTING THE ENVIRONMENT

2 HISTORY   BACK THEN, IN ARKANSAS   28
THE FIRST PEOPLE • BUILDING A TERRITORY • THE CHALLENGES OF STATEHOOD •
SONG: "WE'RE COMING, ARKANSAS" • WAR AND RECONSTRUCTION • THE
TWENTIETH CENTURY • THE LITTLE ROCK NINE • ARKANSAS TOMORROWS

3 GOVERNMENT AND ECONOMY   ARKANSAS AT WORK   50
INSIDE GOVERNMENT • PREVENTING CRIME • EDUCATION AND HUMAN
SERVICES • THE ECONOMY

4 PEOPLE   A PROUD PEOPLE   70
CULTURAL FOUNDATIONS • MOUNTAIN FOLK • RECIPE: ARKANSAS CORN BREAD •
SPIRIT OF THE FRONTIER • DELTA LIFE • THE NEWCOMERS • LEGENDARY
ARKANSAS • FACING THE FUTURE

5 ACHIEVEMENTS   ARKANSAS STANDOUTS   88
THE BASKETBALL SUPERSTAR • THE ACADEMY AWARD WINNER • THE POET •
THE CRUSADING EDITOR • THE MAN IN BLACK • THE PRESIDENT

6 LANDMARKS   THE GRAND TOUR   104
THE DELTA • THE OZARKS • THE WEST AND THE HEARTLAND • THE SOUTHWEST

STATE SURVEY   119
STATE IDENTIFICATIONS • SONG • GEOGRAPHY • TIMELINE • ECONOMY •
CALENDAR OF CELEBRATIONS • STATE STARS • TOUR THE STATE • FUN FACTS

FIND OUT MORE   140

INDEX   142

ARKANSAS IS . . . .

Arkansas is a place . . .

"There's a feeling . . . of being a million miles away from New York instead of a mere 3½-hour plane ride. There doesn't seem to be a rush about much of anything. The air is clean and the hills are so lovely that you want to imprint their beauty in your mind for mental vacations the rest of the year."   —journalist Carla Sanders

. . . and it is people.

"If I could rest anywhere, it would be in Arkansaw, where the men are of the real half-horse, half-alligator breed such as grows nowhere else on the face of the universal earth."
—American frontiersman Davy Crockett

"Arkansas is really neither here nor there, fish nor fowl, south nor west. People in Arkansas don't know whether to pull off their shoes and complain of pellagra [rough skin] or go outside and bust a bronc."   —writer Gregory Jaynes

Arkansans honor the old ways . . .

"Storytelling today is still . . . the amusement of choice on long automobile rides, and on school bus trips that wind through dark hollows coming home late at night. . . . Fishermen sit on gravel bars around a fire at night . . . hunters sit on logs around a campfire under the autumn stars, and Halloween party-goers sit around a fireplace or a lighted candle: these are favorite places for tall tales and scary stories."

—folklorists Richard Young and Judy Dockery Young

. . . and aren't afraid to laugh at themselves.

"Arkansas must be a whole lot older than folks think; it's even mentioned in the Bible. Right there in Genesis it says 'Noah looked out of the ark and saw.'"   —anonymous

"Legend has it that Ink, Arkansas was named by postal officials who filled in a form which asked for the town's new name. The instructions said 'write in ink' and so they did."

—writers Ken Beck and Terry Beck

Arkansas calls itself the Natural State. Its people take pride in their natural resources and their way of life. Arkansans aren't afraid of hard work, but they like to keep things in perspective. Even in the cities, there's an easygoing, good-natured approach to the business of living. In the countryside, life moves at the pace of nature—slowly, with plenty of time to savor the days.

The state has its problems: poverty, joblessness, stormy politics. Government and social service agencies are working to overcome these problems without sacrificing traditional ways of life. This blend of modern concerns and old-fashioned values makes Arkansas one of the most intriguing states in the nation.

1 A GOOD AND PLEASANT LAND

Arkansas is a rich land of many contrasts. Its name comes from a Native American word meaning "south wind." Its beauty and its bounty come from nature.

The state is roughly square in shape, bounded by Missouri to the north, Tennessee and Mississippi to the east, Louisiana to the south, and Texas and Oklahoma to the west. There is a strange notch missing from the northeastern corner. It looks like someone carefully cut out a small piece of Arkansas and left it in Missouri. That is just about what happened.

When the border was being set in 1819, wealthy landowner Colonel John H. Walker didn't want his holdings split between two states. Friends in high places made sure that Colonel Walker's property ended up on the Missouri side—so Arkansas ended up with a notch.

LANDFORMS

Arkansas's landscape varies dramatically, from the green silence of the Ozark Mountains to the steamy Mississippi Delta country. It is divided almost equally between highlands in the northwest and lowlands in the southeast.

The Highland Region. The highlands include the Ozark Plateau, the Ouachita (pronounced WA-sheh-taw) Mountains, and the

LAND AND WATER

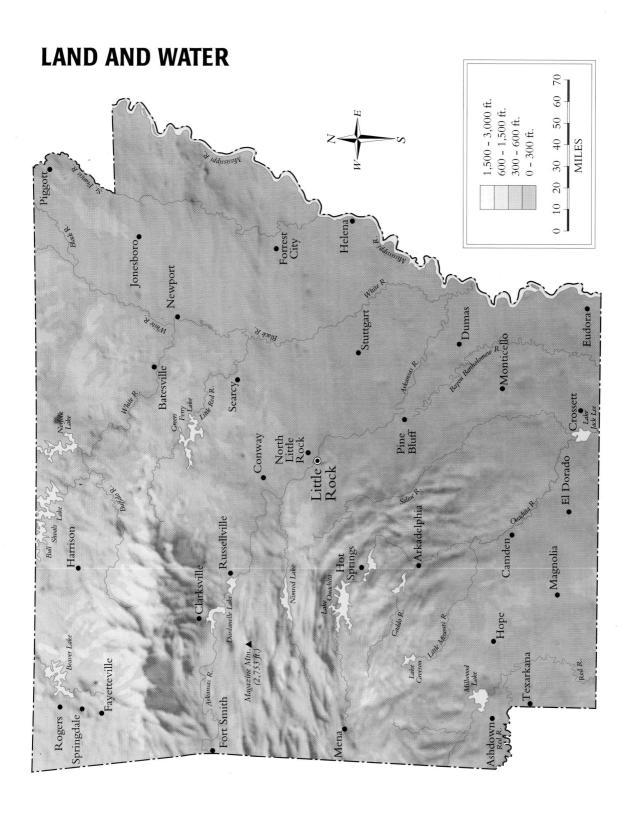

Piggott

St. Francis R.

Black R.

Mississippi R.

Jonesboro

Newport

Forrest City

Helena

White R.

Black R.

White R.

Batesville

Searcy

Greers Ferry Lake

Little Red R.

Stuttgart

Mississippi R.

Dumas

Monticello

Bayou Bartholomew R.

Arkansas R.

Eudora

Norfork Lake

Conway

North Little Rock

Pine Bluff

Crossett

Lake Jack Lee

Bull Shoals Lake

Harrison

Buffalo R.

Russellville

Clarksville

Little Rock

Saline R.

Arkadelphia

Camden

El Dorado

Ouachita R.

Nimrod Lake

Hot Springs

Lake Ouachita

Caddo R.

Magnolia

Beaver Lake

Fayetteville

Dardanelle Lake

Magazine Mtn. ▲
(2,753 ft.)

Little Missouri R.

Hope

Lake Greeson

Millwood Lake

Texarkana

Red R.

Rogers

Springdale

Arkansas R.

Fort Smith

Mena

Ashdown

Red R.

Legend

1,500 – 3,000 ft.
600 – 1,500 ft.
300 – 600 ft.
0 – 300 ft.

MILES

0 10 20 30 40 50 60 70

N E S W

The Ozarks' rocky cliffs and spectacular vistas attract many hikers.

Arkansas River valley, which separates them. The name *Ozark* comes from the French *aux arcs*, which means "at the bows." Nobody seems to know exactly how this name applies. Some say it could refer to the curves and bends in the mountain rivers and trails, or perhaps to the archery bows of Native Americans.

Whatever the origin of the name, the Ozarks are widely regarded as one of the most beautiful areas in the United States. Rugged hills, dotted with caves and sinkholes, rise to the peaks of the Boston Mountains, more than two thousand feet above sea level. After a hike through the Ozarks, backpacker Dennis Thomas said they "look suspiciously like a picture-perfect postcard."

The Ozarks are made up of hollows and knobs. Hollows—or hollers, as the hill folk call them—are deep, narrow valleys carved

In autumn, the Ozarks are ablaze with color.

over countless thousands of years by fast-moving rivers and streams. Knobs are hills with noticeably rounded tops. For newcomer Elliott West, these hills and valleys are a natural paradise: "There are dogwoods, huckleberries, and uncountable wildflowers, creeks, and caves. . . . We can hike for hours, seeing no other people but plenty of hawks . . . woodpeckers, and deer, with occasional wild turkeys, skunks, armadillos, foxes, porcupines. . . . It is a varied landscape, one we will spend our lives getting to know."

The Arkansas River valley is a wide trough, cut by the ceaseless motion of the river. Near the riverbanks, the land is fairly level and suitable for farming. Here and there, the level terrain is interrupted by a lone mountain. Arkansas's tallest peak, Magazine Mountain, rises from this valley.

The Arkansas River valley is bordered on the south by the Ouachita Mountains. The name comes from a Native American word meaning "good hunting grounds." The Ouachitas are a series of ridges and ravines running in an east-west direction.

The Lowland Region. The Arkansas lowlands include the Gulf Coastal Plain in the south and the Mississippi Delta in the east. A third division, Crowley's Ridge, cuts like a jagged scar across the Delta.

The Gulf Coastal Plain spreads up from the Gulf of Mexico into southwestern Arkansas. Dense forests of pine once grew wild on the rolling plain. Today, commercial timber companies plant and manage the forests. The trees thrive in the sandy clay soil.

In the southern part of the Delta lies Bayou Bartholomew, partly in Arkansas and partly in neighboring Louisiana. It is believed to be the longest bayou, or swamp, in the world. The soil is never dry,

The lakes and bayous of Felsenthal National Wildlife Refuge support a wide variety of plant and animal life.

so water-loving grasses, bushes, and trees grow everywhere. Sometimes in the heat, fog clouds rise from the surface. Then the bayou becomes a place of mystery, silent except for animal noises: the croaking of armies of frogs, the call of passing birds, the splashing of an alligator as it slips into a stream.

The Mississippi Delta covers the eastern third of Arkansas, from the Louisiana border all the way up to Missouri. The rich soil, which was deposited there by the flooding of the Mississippi River, is the best farmland in all of Arkansas. Rice, soybeans, and many other crops grow on the flat, fertile land. Crowley's Ridge is perhaps the oddest landform in Arkansas. It is two hundred feet high, two hundred miles long, and so narrow it appears as a startling interruption to the Delta lowlands. This densely forested ridge is covered with a pale yellow powdery substance called loess.

THE CLIMATE

Arkansas has a moderate climate. Statewide, the average temperature is eighty-two degrees in July and forty-five in January. Beyond such general statements, it is difficult to talk about the climate as a whole. In Arkansas, there is highland weather and there is lowland weather. Each region has its own patterns.

The northern highlands average about forty inches of rain each year. March through May is the wettest period. Winter brings twenty-degree temperatures and a dusting of snow to the Ozarks. In autumn, the leaves turn to shades of copper, crimson, and golden yellow.

The southern lowlands receive an average of fifty-five inches of rain per year. In this region, December and January are the wettest months. Winters in southern Arkansas are milder and shorter than those in the north. Summers are hot and humid: temperatures can soar into the nineties and the moisture in the air makes it feel even hotter. "July in the Delta starts feeling like you could grab a handful of air and wring it out like an old waterlogged dishrag," said one Arkansan.

Like other southeastern states, Arkansas suffers from tornadoes, enduring an average of about twenty per year. These violent whirling winds are most common in early spring, when weather

A blanket of snow covers a farm in the Ozarks.

patterns are changing. Some tornadoes do a great deal of damage. In April 1996, for example, a tornado struck Fort Smith, near the Oklahoma border. It swept through the downtown area, then hit the residential community of Van Buren. Two children died in that storm. More than three thousand houses and one hundred businesses were destroyed. The following year, twenty-four people died in a tornado that slashed across the state.

WATERWAYS

The two main rivers passing through Arkansas are the Mississippi and the Arkansas. The Mississippi forms Arkansas's eastern border, except for the notch in the northeastern corner. The Arkansas River flows through the highland valley that shares its name, crossing the state to join the Mississippi. Other important rivers are the White River in the northeast, the Ouachita River in the west, and the Red River, which forms part of the border with Texas.

Arkansas also has a wealth of streams, many with colorful names like Strawberry, Crooked Creek, War Eagle, and Big Piney. Streams are not as wide or as deep as larger rivers, and they do not cover as much territory. Because their water rushes through narrow channels, streams don't move with the stately grandeur of big rivers. Instead, they usually flow quickly, and in steep, mountainous terrain they crash, dash, and explode into great white-water froths.

The Buffalo National River in the Ozarks was the first stream placed under federal government protection. This beautiful 150-mile-long stream plunges down two thousand feet of mountainside, through limestone bluffs and dense forests, to join with the White River.

Arkansas is famous for its springs. The headwaters of the Spring River are at Mammoth Spring, one of the largest springs in the world. Nearly ten million gallons of water flow out of it every hour. Arkansas has a number of hot mineral springs in the Ouachita

A trip down the Buffalo National River will take you past towering cliffs and waterfalls.

Mountains. The best-known of these sites is Hot Springs, where there are forty-seven naturally heated springs.

Arkansas has many lakes, both natural and artificial. Lake Chicot in the Mississippi Delta is the largest natural lake in the state. It is an oxbow lake, a type of lake that was originally a sharp bend in a river, but was cut off when the river changed course. Most artificial lakes in Arkansas were created by damming rivers. These dams can provide water storage, aid in flood control, or even generate hydroelectric power. Among the state's most important artificial lakes are Lakes Ouachita and Catherine on the Ouachita

Lake Ouachita, Arkansas's largest lake, is known for its crystal clear water.

Tulip trees can grow 150 feet tall. Their large flowers appear in late spring and early summer in the branches high up in the tree.

River, Dardanelle Lake on the Arkansas River, and Beaver Lake on the White River.

PLANTS AND ANIMALS

Arkansas is rich with living things. More than half the state is forested. Hardwoods such as ash, hickory, maple, and oak grow in the northern part of the state. In the southwest, there are softwood forests, mostly loblolly and shortleaf pine. Flowering tulip trees, also known as yellow poplars, grow on Crowley's Ridge.

Other flowering trees and shrubs include dogwood, redbud, and azalea. In springtime, the trees blossom and wildflowers carpet meadows, hillsides, and riverbanks. Arkansas has bluebells and hydrangeas, water lilies and sweet-smelling yellow jasmine. The lady's slipper, a species of wild orchid, grows in the pine forests of the Gulf Coastal Plain.

Arkansas has many species of birds, including robins, mocking-birds, phoebes, and cardinals. The distinctive call of the whippoorwill often sounds through the Ozark night.

Fish such as bass, catfish, and perch populate the lakes and streams. Lobsterlike crawfish, or "mudbugs" as they are called in Arkansas, are abundant in the Delta.

Among the animals in the state's forests are raccoons, skunks, weasels, woodchucks, foxes, rabbits, and deer. The animal most closely associated with Arkansas is probably the razorback hog. This wild boar, described by one Arkansan as "a couple hundred pounds of mean and ugly, with bristles down its back," is the University of Arkansas mascot. When Razorback fans cheer their sports teams, they do it with an old-time Arkansas hog call: "Woo, Pig, Souie! / Woo, Pig, Souie! / Woo, Pig, Souie! / Razorbacks!"

PROTECTING THE ENVIRONMENT

Arkansas takes environmental protection seriously. Everybody gets involved: government, business and industry, and private citizens. In 1997, the Arkansas legislature created a special loan fund for environmental projects in private industry. Small businesses could now borrow money to improve their environmental protection programs. For example, a manufacturer could get a loan to build a

Crayfish, sometimes called mudbugs, often burrow into the muddy banks of streams and rivers.

Raccoons thrive in Arkansas's forests.

BATS!

Arkansas is home to three species of bats that are endangered: the gray bat, the Indiana bat, and the Ozark big-eared bat.

Ozark big-eared bats are well named: their ears are huge, their faces comically fierce. Only about three hundred Ozark big-eareds remain in Arkansas. They live in two Ozark caves; they hibernate in one and have babies in the other. The U.S. government owns the hibernation cave; the maternity cave is on private property. The property owner has agreed to protect the bat "nursery" so that mothers and babies will be undisturbed.

Gray bats are often tiny, sometimes weighing as little as a quarter ounce. Their colonies used to occupy several caves in Arkansas. Now, only one hibernation cave remains. It is home to about 250,000 of the little mammals. Gray bats have been listed as endangered since 1976, but their numbers are now increasing.

Indiana bats hibernate in clusters. As many as 480 have been counted in one square foot of space. Fewer than three thousand Indiana bats remain in Arkansas.

The main reason the number of bats has fallen is that their caves have been disturbed or vandalized. The chief method of protecting them is by keeping humans out of their habitats. One major hibernation cave in the Ozarks has been fenced off, and signs have been posted in four others, warning the public to keep out. Hopefully, these efforts will help bats make a comeback in Arkansas.

system to filter the pollutants it emits into the air, or a company that makes pollution-control technologies could borrow funds to develop new products.

Ordinary people are also involved in keeping the environment

Kids help clean up Greers Ferry Lake.

clean. Environmental "housekeeping" is a proud tradition in Arkansas. Signs all over the state remind people to FIGHT DIRTY! KEEP ARKANSAS CLEAN. Parks throughout the state host Great Arkansas Cleanup days. On these days, hundreds of Arkansans turn out to pick up litter from trails and campsites and fish it out of lakes and streams. Volunteers get a free lunch and the satisfaction of knowing they made a difference.

2 BACK THEN, IN ARKANSAS

Twin Falls of the Devil's Fork, by William McNamara

When Spanish explorer Hernando de Soto first saw Arkansas in 1541, he was looking for gold. He gave up after a year, having found none. Nearly 150 years later, the French explored the region. In 1682, René-Robert Cavelier, Sieur de La Salle, traveled down the Mississippi to its mouth. He claimed the area for France and named it Louisiana in honor of King Louis XIV.

France ceded the Louisiana territory to Spain in 1762. Spain ceded it back to France in 1800. Three years later, the United States bought it from France in the famous Louisiana Purchase of 1803. Arkansas was part of the bargain.

THE FIRST PEOPLE

Native Americans had been in Arkansas for thousands of years before Europeans arrived. Among the prehistoric peoples who lived there were the Bluff Dwellers and the Mound Builders. The Bluff Dwellers lived in caves and rock shelters. They were nomads who wandered from place to place, feeding themselves off the bounty of the land. The men hunted game while the women gathered edible plants. The Mound Builders were hunters and farmers, who built enormous mounds of hard-packed earth. Sometimes they used these mounds as foundations for their buildings.

The descendants of these prehistoric peoples were the Quapaw,

The Quapaw Indians were both hunters and farmers.

Osage, and Caddo tribal groups. They were already well established in Arkansas when Europeans arrived. The Caddo lived in the south-western part of the state, while the Osage settled in the Ozarks. The Quapaw made their homes on the lower Arkansas River, near where it flows into the Mississippi.

The Osage, Caddo, and Quapaw were skilled hunters. They also grew such crops as corn, beans, and squash. The Caddo lived in large rounded thatched cottages, each of which housed many families. Although each family had its own area, they shared a central fire, which was never allowed to go out. The Quapaw built dwellings of earth and covered them with bark, while the Osage

When the world was young, people lived forever. At first, this seemed a fine thing; but after a time, Earth ran out of room. New people could not be born, because there was no place for them to live. The chiefs got together to decide what to do about this problem. One said that maybe everybody should have to die for a little while, so there wouldn't be so many people on Earth all at once.

This would never work, Coyote said. If all the people who died came back, there wouldn't be enough food to feed them all. The chiefs considered this, but they could not bring themselves to make anyone die forever. They built a house of grass, facing east, toward the rising sun. Here, they would call the spirit to enter the house and become alive again.

After the first man died, medicine men gathered in the grass house to call his spirit home. They called until a spirit-wind came and whirled around the grass house. Just as it reached the doorway, Coyote jumped up and closed the door. Finding no way to get inside, the spirit-wind blew on by and soon was gone. The man who had died never returned. This is how Coyote brought death into the world and made it last forever.

erected frameworks of saplings and covered them with woven mats.

White immigration gradually forced Arkansas's Native Americans off their tribal lands. Since 1835, when the Caddo were forced west of Arkansas's borders, there have been no tribal lands in the state.

BUILDING A TERRITORY

The first European settlement in what would become Arkansas

Henri de Tonti founded the first European settlement in what would become Arkansas.

was founded in 1686 by Henri de Tonti, a member of the La Salle expedition. Only six people lived in this community, which later became known as Arkansas Post. For more than a hundred years, Arkansas was not widely settled by Europeans. As late as 1799, only 386 white people lived there.

In 1819, Arkansas became an official territory of the United States. Its boundaries were much the same as they are today, except on the west. Territorial Arkansas contained part of what is now Oklahoma.

As a young man, William E. Woodruff, a native New Yorker, decided to move west. In 1819, he ended up in Arkansas Post, where he founded Arkansas's first newspaper, the Arkansas Gazette.

That same year, an ambitious young printer named William E. Woodruff arrived at Arkansas Post. He had decided that the new territory needed a print shop and a newspaper of its own. On November 20, 1819, he put out the first issue of the *Arkansas Gazette*. When the territorial capital was transferred from Arkansas Post to the new town of Little Rock, Woodruff and the Gazette went along. It was the beginning of a genuine, homegrown Arkansas institution. The *Arkansas Gazette* lasted for 172 years— its final issue went to press on October 18, 1991.

The *Gazette* shaped public opinion in many ways. For example, the territory had been called Akansea, Acansa, Akansas, and

Arkansaw as well as Arkansas. Woodruff settled the matter with a minimum of fuss. He simply made sure that the *Gazette* used nothing but "Arkansas," and before long that became the favored spelling.

Pronunciation was another issue. Was it AR-kan-SAW in the French manner, or KAN-sas with an "Ar" in front of it? Even politicians couldn't agree. At one point, the disagreement carried all the way to the floor of the United States Senate, where one senator was always introduced as the senator from AR-kan-SAW, and the other as the senator from Ar-KAN-sas. The question wasn't officially answered until 1881, when the state legislature passed a resolution making "Arkansas" the official spelling, and AR-kan-SAW the pronunciation.

THE CHALLENGES OF STATEHOOD

Throughout the 1820s, more settlers came to Arkansas. Families built homes. Townships planned courthouses and city halls. Gristmills and sawmills were scattered throughout the territory, and cotton farms were springing up in the South. By 1830, Arkansas had a population of 30,388. It was admitted to the Union on June 15, 1836, becoming the twenty-fifth state of the young republic.

Like most frontier societies, Arkansas was rough, wild, and often lawless. Occasional scandals marked the early years of statehood. Shortly after becoming mayor of Little Rock, Samuel G. Trowbridge was arrested for burglary and counterfeiting money. "His Honor" turned out to be the mastermind behind a gang of criminals operating in the Little Rock area.

WE'RE COMING, ARKANSAS

They say that a proposal was once introduced in the state legislature to change the name of Arkansas. No one knows whether this actually happened. Nevertheless, speeches purported to have been made in response to the proposal

are part of Arkansas folklore: "Compare the valley to a gorgeous sunrise; the discordant croak of the bullfrog to the melodious tones of a nightingale; the classic strains of Mozart to the bray of a Mexican mule . . . but never change the name of Arkansas."

four-horse team will soon be seen on the road to Ark - an - sas.

The men keep hounds down there,
And hunting is all they care;
The women plough and hoe the corn,
While the men shoot turkey and deer. *Chorus*

The girls are strong down there,
Clean and healthy and gay,
They card and spin from morning till night
And dance from night till day. *Chorus*

They raise their 'baccer patch,
The women all smoke and chaw,
Eat hog, and hominy and poke for greens
Way down in Arkansas. *Chorus*

The roads are tough down there,
You must take um 'done or raw'
There's rocks and rills and stumps and hills
On the road to Arkansas. *Chorus*

In this frontier society, even basically honest officials did things that would not be acceptable today. Beginning in the 1820s, three families dominated Arkansas politics: the Seviers, the Conways, and the Johnsons. They appointed relatives and close friends to important positions and handpicked their candidates for elective offices.

In 1836, William Woodruff resigned as editor of the *Gazette* in order to enter state government. As a strong ally of the three families, he became Arkansas's first state treasurer. In that position, he expected to receive a commission on land sold for back taxes and to have a free hand with his expense account. He received a rude awakening when the legislature disallowed his commission on the sale of land along with almost half of his expenses. Instead of making money from the treasurer's office, the disappointed Woodruff ended up owing the state more than two thousand dollars for excess expenses. He chose not to run for another term.

Despite its political troubles, Arkansas grew. In 1840, the state had a population of more than 97,000 people. Nearly 20,000 of them were slaves. By this time, the Northern states had outlawed slavery, but the South had not. Its plantation culture was based on cotton farming, which required a plentiful supply of cheap labor. Northern abolitionists (activists who worked to end slavery) argued that slavery was inhumane, but Southern slave owners refused to yield. The conflict triggered the bloodiest war in American history.

WAR AND RECONSTRUCTION

On April 12, 1861, Southern military forces attacked the U.S. Army

Thousands of young Arkansans like these joined the Confederate army.

garrison at Fort Sumter, South Carolina. The Civil War had begun.

Before this strike, South Carolina and seven other states had seceded from the Union to form the Confederate States of America. In May, Arkansas followed their lead, becoming the ninth state to join the Confederacy.

Not everyone in Arkansas supported the Confederacy. In the mountains and high valleys of the northern part of the state, few people owned slaves, or cared to own them. Many of these people supported the Union, or at least did not actively oppose it. Fifteen thousand young Arkansans joined the Union army, while 60,000 fought for the Confederacy.

Arkansans with Confederate sympathies threw themselves into "the cause." For some, this meant nothing more risky than raising money for the war effort. For others, it meant the ultimate sacrifice.

Arkansans still tell the story of David Owen Dodd. He was just seventeen years old when Union troops captured him near Little Rock. An innocent-looking notebook in his pocket contained a coded report on enemy troop strength in the area. Dodd was found guilty of spying and was sentenced to hang. Union general Frederick Steele offered a pardon in exchange for the names of others who helped gather the information. "I can die, but I cannot betray the trust of a friend," Dodd is said to have replied. He was hanged on schedule and later took his place in Arkansas legend as "the boy martyr of the Confederacy."

In the end, heroism and dedication to the cause were not enough. By late 1863, Union forces occupied most of Arkansas. The Confederacy was finally defeated in 1865. For Arkansans returning from the war, a new struggle lay ahead. Veterans found their farms destroyed, their livestock and equipment gone, and their credit lost. Former slaves struggled to make a place for themselves in society. This was the beginning of Reconstruction. During this period, which lasted until 1877, the states of the former Confederacy were gradually brought back into the Union.

In Arkansas, as in the rest of the South, Reconstruction was a time of economic hardship, political corruption, and public uncertainty. Immediately after the war the state legislature, which was composed largely of former Confederates, passed laws to restrict the freedom of former slaves. The Union army put a stop to this practice by

CELEBRATING HISTORY

Festivals with historic themes are popular in Arkansas. Every October, the town of Evening Shade holds the Annual Founder's Day and Pioneer Rendezvous, which transforms the modern town into a frontier settlement of 1847. The local folk dress in period costume and encourage visitors to do the same. People come to town on horseback or in wagons to listen to old-time, foot-stomping music and to sample homemade goodies from an enormous dessert table.

The Annual Civil War Weekend at Lake Chicot State Park is living history at its best. The event features complete and detailed Confederate and Union army camps, demonstrations of Civil War artillery and firearms, and music and dancing from the period. The climax of the three-day event is a reenactment of the Battle at Ditch Bayou.

placing Arkansas under military rule. Home rule was not fully restored until Arkansas passed a new state constitution in 1874. Even then, African Americans did not have equal rights. The law was one thing; reality was another. Race remained a defining issue for Arkansas and the rest of the Old South.

A generation after the Civil War ended slavery, a series of new laws established racial segregation in the south. These Jim Crow laws, named after a popular minstrel show character, divided the South into two distinct groups: one white, the other black. Hotels, cafés, theaters, public bathrooms, and even water fountains were segregated. An African American who drank at a "whites only" fountain or entered a "whites only" rest room could be arrested as a criminal.

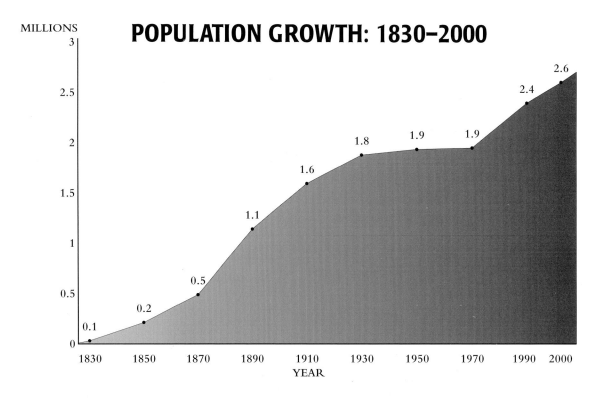

POPULATION GROWTH: 1830–2000

MILLIONS

(Chart showing population growth values by year)

- 1830: 0.1
- 1850: 0.2
- 1870: 0.5
- 1890: 1.1
- 1910: 1.6
- 1930: 1.8
- 1950: 1.9
- 1970: 1.9
- 1990: 2.4
- 2000: 2.6

YEAR

THE TWENTIETH CENTURY

By 1900, Arkansas had a population of 1.3 million people, the majority of them employed in agriculture. Industrialization and modernization lagged behind much of the country until 1921, when oil was discovered in the southern part of the state, near the town of El Dorado. Suddenly, office buildings, hotels, schools, and electric lines sprang up all over the state. Roads that had been dirt trails became paved highways.

This modernization was interrupted in 1927, when the Mississippi River flooded. One writer called it "the greatest flood since

Noah's." It left thousands homeless, hundreds dead, and whole towns utterly destroyed.

Nature was not through with Arkansas. Three years after the flood, there was a drought. Crops withered in the fields, and topsoil blew away in great swirls of wind.

In what Arkansans might call "piling on the agony," the stock

Until the twentieth century, Arkansas's economy was dependent on such crops as cotton.

In the 1920s, the discovery of oil in southern Arkansas created jobs for thousands of young men.

market crashed in 1929. The resulting Great Depression threw the whole country into economic chaos. Arkansas suffered along with the rest of the nation. Farmers lost their land, families lost their homes, and thousands of hardworking people lost their jobs.

In time, the drought ended, as did the Depression, but they were replaced by the horrors of war. The United States entered World War II in 1941. By the time the war ended in 1945, 200,000 young Arkansans had gone into the armed services. Many of them came home with new ideas. For African Americans, those new ideas helped to trigger the civil rights movement. In Arkansas and the rest of the South, Jim Crow segregation was about to come to an end.

THE LITTLE ROCK NINE

On September 25, 1997, nine middle-aged African Americans walked together to the front door of Central High School in Little Rock. They were met by applause and flashing cameras. President Bill Clinton and Arkansas governor Mike Huckabee made speeches praising their courage.

On this date forty years earlier, Ernest Green, Melba Patillo,

The Great Depression caused terrible hardship for people across Arkansas. Here, sharecroppers are evicted from their homes in Cross County.

Minnijean Brown, Thelma Mothershed, Gloria Ray, Terrance Roberts, Carlotta Walls, Jefferson Thomas, and Elizabeth Eckford had made civil rights history, breaking the color barrier at previously all-white Central High.

Of these nine, Elizabeth Eckford is perhaps best remembered. She was fifteen at the time, bright, pretty, and eager for a good education. On September 4, 1957, she walked alone through the screaming mob that stood between her and the front door of the school. When she tried to enter, Arkansas National Guardsmen barred the way. Press photographer Will Counts captured Elizabeth's bravery on film. The image of that young girl, alone in a sea of hatred, stirred the conscience of the nation. In 1997

Approaching Little Rock's Central High School on the first day of class, Elizabeth Eckford says, "was the longest block I ever walked in my whole life."

President Bill Clinton, himself an Arkansan, talked about that dark day: "We saw not one nation under God, indivisible, with liberty and justice for all, but two Americas, divided and unequal. What happened here changed the course of our country."

While Elizabeth faced the mob, the other eight students were gathering a few blocks away. The Arkansas National Association for the Advancement of Colored People had arranged for the teenagers to go to school as a group. Somehow, Elizabeth never got the word.

The eight other students also tried to enter the school that day, with the same result. In the days that followed, judges would make rulings, racists would burn crosses on people's lawns, and President Dwight D. Eisenhower would send in the U.S. Army to protect the students and keep the peace. Twenty-one days after Elizabeth Eckford was turned away, the Little Rock Nine finally walked through the schoolhouse door.

Despite the army escort, it was a frightening day for the nine young people. "All I could hear was my own heartbeat and the sound of boots clicking on stone," recalled Melba Patillo Beals. For many white onlookers, who grew up accepting racism as a normal part of life, September 25 was a day of horror. According to reporter Relman Morin, as the nine mounted the steps, white women in the crowd were crying to police officers, "They are in our school, Oh God, are you going to stand there and let them stay in school?"

In the midst of this fury, the Little Rock Nine tended to business. When they walked through the door of Central High, their struggle became part of civil rights history, and the students themselves became genuine Arkansas heroes. Arkansas has made progress since

Three of the Little Rock Nine—Terrance Roberts, Carlotta Walls LaNier, and Ernest Green—with President Bill Clinton and First Lady Hillary Rodham Clinton commemorating the integration of Central High. "Forty years ago today," the president said, the nine "climbed these steps, passed through this door, and moved our nation. And for that, we must all thank them.

those desperate days in 1957. Race relations still have a long way to go, but official segregation in the public schools is a thing of the past.

ARKANSAS TOMORROWS

In recent years, Arkansas has become more urban and industrial than the early settlers could have ever imagined. It is now home to successful nationwide companies such as Wal-Mart and Tyson Foods.

As it moves into the twenty-first century, Arkansas has not lost touch with its past. The folk cultures that may once have seemed backward and hopelessly old-fashioned have become sources of pride. Tourists come from all over the nation and the world to experience these traditions, and to enjoy the state's natural beauty. For their part, many Arkansans have decided that living in a place where the end of the world "wouldn't arrive . . . until twenty years later" suits them just fine.

3 ARKANSAS AT WORK

The capitol in Little Rock

In Arkansas, even the highest levels of government and industry function with a kind of down-home coziness. When President Bill Clinton was governor of Arkansas, he spoke about this closeness: "In my state, when people lose their jobs, there's a good chance I'll know them by their names. When a factory closes, I know the people who ran it. When the businesses go bankrupt, I know them."

In the computer age, Arkansas leaders are blending old-fashioned neighborliness with the latest in high-tech communications. The goal is to make government more responsive to the people.

INSIDE GOVERNMENT

Arkansas's state government follows the federal model, with three independent but interrelated branches: executive, legislative, and judicial.

Executive. The governor is chief executive officer of the state. He or she serves a four-year term, with a two-term limit on the number of terms that can be served. The governor draws up the state's budget, appoints members to various departments and commissions, and proposes laws and economic programs to the legislature.

Other positions in the executive branch include lieutenant

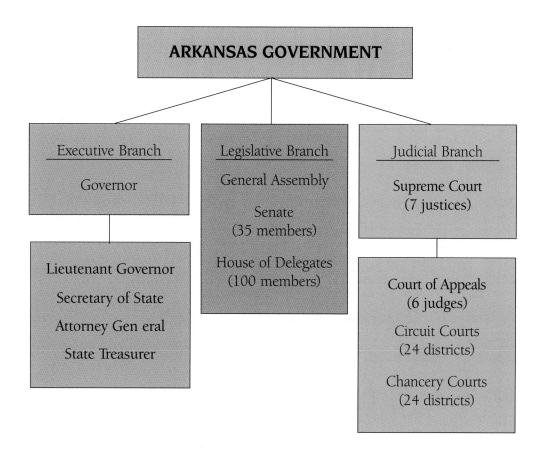

ARKANSAS GOVERNMENT

Executive Branch

Governor

Lieutenant Governor

Secretary of State

Attorney Gen eral

State Treasurer

Legislative Branch

General Assembly

Senate
(35 members)

House of Delegates
(100 members)

Judicial Branch

Supreme Court
(7 justices)

Court of Appeals
(6 judges)

Circuit Courts
(24 districts)

Chancery Courts
(24 districts)

governor, secretary of state, treasurer, auditor, and attorney general.

Most of Arkansas's governors have belonged to the Democratic Party. In the entire history of the state, only seven Republicans have occupied the governor's office. Four of them served during the period of Reconstruction that followed the Civil War.

Not until 1967 would another Republican occupy the state-house. Winthrop Rockefeller seemed an unlikely choice for the job. Not only was he a Republican but he was also a northerner and a member of one of the richest families in America. He came to Arkansas because he had investments in the state, and he stayed because he liked the pace of life.

In 1967, Winthrop Rockefeller of the famous New York Rockefeller family became the first Republican governor of Arkansas in nearly a century.

His grandfather was the legendary John D. Rockefeller, one of the founders of Standard Oil. His brother Nelson was governor of New York and would later become vice president of the United States under Gerald Ford. Winthrop Rockefeller served two terms as governor. After losing his bid for a third term in 1970, he moved to Palm Springs, California. He died there in 1973.

The Rockefeller family's association with Arkansas did not end with Winthrop Rockefeller's death. His son, Winthrop Paul Rockefeller, became lieutenant governor in 1996.

Legislative. Arkansas's state legislature, the General Assembly, is made up of a senate with thirty-five members, and a house of representatives with one hundred members. State senators serve four-year terms, while representatives serve two years.

The legislature makes the laws for the state. Committees such as education, public health, and economic development study proposed laws in their particular areas. For example, the education committee might debate standards for teacher certification; the economic development committee might propose laws to help people start new businesses in the state. When a committee sends a bill (proposed law) to the full legislature, it must pass both the house and the senate before it is sent to the governor to be signed into law.

Service in Arkansas's legislature is part time. Most senators and representatives have full-time jobs outside of government service. For example, in 1997, the state senate included lawyers, educators, cattlemen, and insurance agents, along with a car dealer, a forester, and the owner of a Wendy's restaurant.

Judicial. The Arkansas supreme court is the state's highest court. The supreme court has a chief justice and six associate justices, who are elected for eight-year terms. Until 1978, the supreme court was the only appellate court in the state. Anyone who wanted to challenge a ruling of a lower court had nowhere else to go.

When the workload became too heavy, the state created a six-judge court of appeals. Now, most appeals go to the court of appeals, which hands down a decision. In many cases, the appeal ends there. If the person filing the appeal is still not satisfied, he or she may request a hearing before the state supreme court. Cases that involve a possible death penalty or require an interpretation of the state consitution go directly to the supreme court. These two courts have developed a fast-track system for hearing cases. In many states, an appeal can take months. In Arkansas, the goal is two weeks from the filing of an appeal to a judicial decision.

Arkansas's main trial courts are circuit, or district, courts. More than one hundred judges, who are elected for four-year terms, preside over these courts. Beneath this level, chancery courts handle domestic cases and other civil matters. There are also county courts and municipal (city) courts to deal with justice on a local level.

PREVENTING CRIME

Arkansas has an active crime prevention program, which gets government agencies and ordinary citizens involved in stopping crime before it happens. The state police make background checks on applicants for gun permits, in order to keep firearms away from known criminals. The Office of Crime Prevention furnishes educational materials and offers training in methods of preventing crime, such as neighborhood watch programs and special programs for children and senior citizens.

EDUCATION AND HUMAN SERVICES

Arkansas has a solid system of schools and human services. Though the budget for these services is limited, Arkansas has used it well. For example, the Division of Children and Family Services uses the Internet to seek adoptive families for hard-to-place children. Its website includes a photo and biography of each child, explaining his or her situation and needs.

One of the most exciting programs in Arkansas's school system is the magnet school. These schools specialize in certain subjects and draw students interested in those subjects from across district lines. Crystal Hill Elementary Magnet School in North Little Rock is a good example. Its subject area is communications. Students at Crystal Hill learn about computers and the Internet, produce their own videotape projects, and learn how to use other communications technologies. They also study more traditional subjects related to communications, such as photography, journalism, dramatics, and public speaking.

Horace Mann Magnet Junior High School is in Little Rock's east end. It became an arts and sciences junior high in 1987. At Horace Mann, art students can study visual arts, drama, dance, and music,

GROSS STATE PRODUCT: $63.7 BILLION

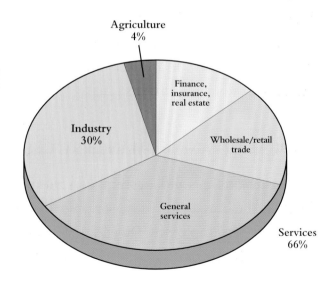

Agriculture 4%

Finance, insurance, real estate

Industry 30%

Wholesale/retail trade

General services

Services 66%

(2000 estimated)

Arkansas students visit the statehouse.

while science students get to work in an experimental laboratory. The school draws talented students from across the city. "There are more opportunities to do stuff here. It's more hands-on than other schools," said student Andrea Anderson. "I came here because I wanted to be in band," said Fred McKindra. "The band director is one of the best in Arkansas."

THE ECONOMY

Arkansas is not a wealthy state. In 1996, Arkansas's average household income was ranked forty-seventh among the states. Nor is income distributed evenly around the state. Much of the prosperity is in the northwestern and central part of the state; much of the poverty is in the Mississippi Delta.

The Delta is farm country. The countryside is dotted with the ramshackle cabins of farmers who work the land but do not own it. These people work hard for little reward. "I do whatever they tell me to do—drive the tractor, work with the airplane that sprays the fields, chop the cotton," said one woman. "I do it because I want to work, and I've got to make out the best way I can."

The top three field crops in Arkansas—cotton, rice, and soybeans—all grow well in the Delta. Livestock plays a major role in Arkansas agriculture, particularly in the northwest. Sixty percent of Arkansas's agricultural income comes from cattle, hogs, eggs, and other livestock products. Tyson Foods is the nation's largest producer of chicken products.

The Gulf Coastal Plain of southern Arkansas is the center of a thriving forest products industry. Union and Columbia Counties,

Poverty continues to plague Arkansas, which has one of the lowest average incomes in the nation.

near the Louisiana border, are home to a small but prosperous petroleum industry. Other important minerals produced in Arkansas are bromide, natural gas, and coal.

Much of Arkansas's industry is connected in some way to its wealth of raw materials. The state produces food products, wood products, petrochemicals, and textiles. Arkansas is also the head-

CELEBRATING THE FRUITS OF THE EARTH

Like most farming folk, Arkansans love to celebrate the crops they grow. Festivals allow farmers to show off their produce, cooks to invent new recipes, and visitors to sing, dance, enter races and silly contests, and above all, to eat. In October, harvest festivals are held all over the state.

In the state's northwestern corner, the Arkansas Apple Festival promises a regular feast of apples. Visitors can have apples "sliced, diced, pared & whole; in pies, cobblers & cider or made into any kind of art or craft." There's also country music, square dancing, and a parade.

In the rice fields of the Delta, a rice festival is held each year. It features live entertainment, games, crafts, and a three-on-three hoop shoot. The high point of the celebration is the All Rice Luncheon, which offers diners a choice of 350 different dishes made from rice.

In the Ozark foothills, it's pumpkins. The Annual Pumpkin Festival in the town of Ozark has the usual games and entertainment, along with pumpkin pie, pumpkin custard, pumpkin bread, and pumpkin cake. Of course, no pumpkin festival would be complete without a pumpkin-decorating contest. The local folk create lavish yard displays that range from funny to weird to beautiful.

Almost a million acres of cotton are harvested in Arkansas every year.

Dairy farms are sprinkled across central and northwestern Arkansas.

Arkansans produce a wide variety of food, including pickles.

Although catfish still populate Arkansas's lakes and rivers, the ones you eat in restaurants likely came from a farm such as this.

WHAT THE FARMER FOUND

In 1906, John Huddleston was dirt poor and slowly starving on a hardscrabble farm near Murfreesboro. He was ready to abandon the land when he found a strange, crystal-like stone that changed his life.

It was a diamond. Huddleston's worthless farm sat atop the only diamond mine in North America. Over the years, 70,000 diamonds have been found in the Crater of Diamonds, as the mine has come to be called. Most have been small, industrial-grade stones, but along the way there have been a few stones big enough to name. The forty-carat Uncle Sam, the sixteen-carat Amarillo Starlight, and the fifteen-carat Star of Arkansas were all found in the crater.

Today, the Crater of Diamonds is a state park. For a $4.50 admission fee ($2.00 for children), visitors can dig for diamonds to their hearts' content. The park rangers rent out digging equipment and give prospecting tips for free. Any diamonds you find, you keep.

MINE SHAFT BUILDING

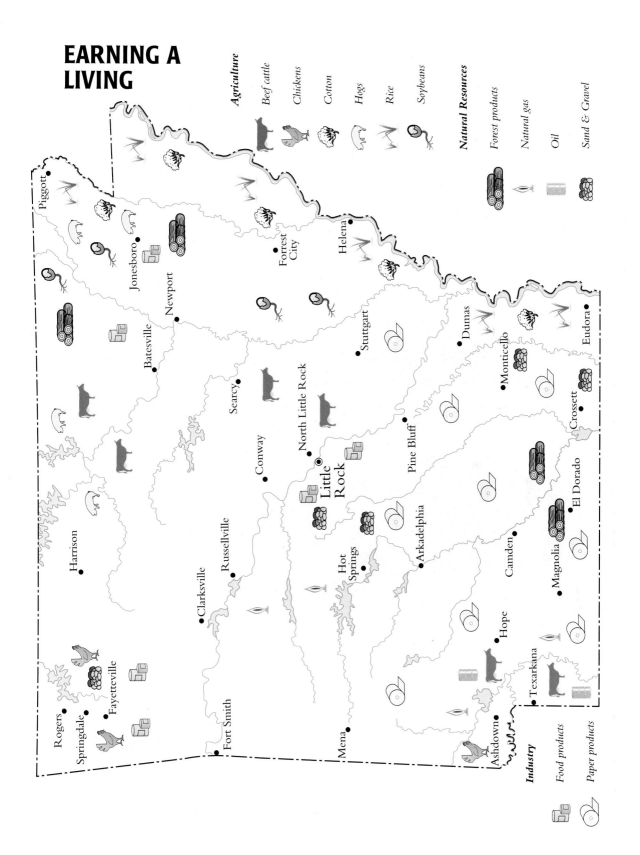

EARNING A LIVING

Agriculture

Beef cattle

Chickens

Cotton

Hogs

Rice

Soybeans

Natural Resources

Forest products

Natural gas

Oil

Sand & Gravel

Industry

Food products

Paper products

Piggott

Jonesboro

Newport

Forrest City

Helena

Batesville

Searcy

Stuttgart

Dumas

Monticello

Eudora

Crossett

North Little Rock

Conway

Little Rock

Pine Bluff

El Dorado

Harrison

Russellville

Arkadelphia

Camden

Magnolia

Clarksville

Hot Springs

Hope

Rogers

Springdale

Fayetteville

Fort Smith

Mena

Ashdown

Texarkana

Little Rock, Arkansas's capital and largest city, is also the state's economic center.

quarters of such major businesses as the huge Wal-Mart chain of retail stores and Beverly Enterprises, the largest chain of nursing homes in the country.

Major industries tend to cluster around larger cities such as Little Rock, Fort Smith, and Fayetteville. Other parts of the state do not fare so well in attracting industry—and the jobs that go with it. In the southwest and in the Delta, jobs outside of agriculture are hard to find. For example, the closing of a Reynolds metal plant in the tiny town of Gum Springs threw nearly five hundred people out of work. Within eighteen months, two other plants also closed. Many workers were forced to move away, searching for work wherever they could find it. Gum Springs eventually recovered some of the jobs it had lost, but not before the closings disrupted thousands of lives.

TEN LARGEST CITIES

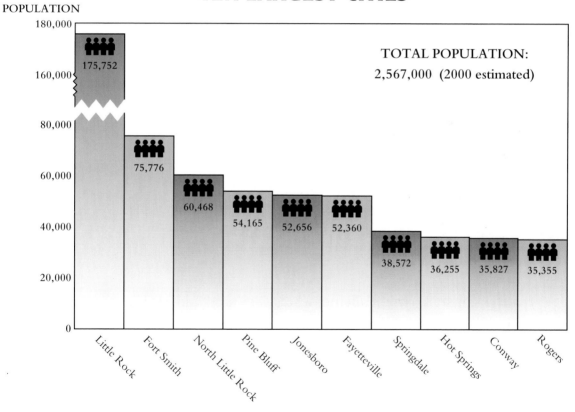

POPULATION

TOTAL POPULATION: 2,567,000 (2000 estimated)

City	Population
Little Rock	175,752
Fort Smith	75,776
North Little Rock	60,468
Pine Bluff	54,165
Jonesboro	52,656
Fayetteville	52,360
Springdale	38,572
Hot Springs	36,255
Conway	35,827
Rogers	35,355

When electronics giant Sanyo decided to close its plant in the Delta town of Forrest City, then-governor Bill Clinton moved quickly to save hundreds of jobs. He contacted Sam Walton, billionaire owner of Wal-Mart stores. Would Wal-Mart agree to buy a certain number of televisions each year, if Sanyo agreed to keep the plant open? Sam Walton said yes, and Bill Clinton flew to Japan for talks with Sanyo. He came home with an agreement that saved hundreds of jobs.

Tourism is an important part of Arkansas's economy, and the state is hoping to make it more so. In 1997, the state began giving tax breaks to investors who planned to build tourist attractions in the state. "If we sit around and wait until we get Disney World, we're not going to get anything done," said tourism director Richard Davies. "But if we start building and getting some stuff going, it will grow on itself."

Growth is what Arkansas needs. For all its natural beauty and human resources, it is still a poor state. In order to break out of the trap of poverty, Arkansas needs a solid program of economic and social development to carry it into the twenty-first century.

Attracting visitors to Arkansas's beautiful countryside is vital to the state's economy.

4 A PROUD PEOPLE

Tradition is important in Arkansas. People feel connected to the land, to one another, and to values they consider timeless. The result is a society that is comfortable with itself, and not much concerned with being trendy. In a changing world, many people want that kind of stability.

"No matter how far away you go, or how famous you get, there's always Arkansas," says one long-time resident. "You can come back home, and it won't be all that different from when you left."

CULTURAL FOUNDATIONS

A large majority of Arkansas's people are of Irish, Scottish, German, and English ancestry. They share similar religious beliefs, political opinions, and ethical values. The result is a stable social system, but one that is slow to change.

Arkansans built their lives around old-fashioned values: hard work, honesty, fierce independence, and unwavering religious faith. Poverty is no reason for shame, so long as it is not caused by laziness, cussedness (a disagreeable nature), or some other personal flaw.

Christian fundamentalists, who believe that everything in the Bible is literally true, have a great deal of influence on political and social life in Arkansas. As late as 1980, then-governor Frank White was able to push through a law requiring public schools to teach

Arkansans of Scottish descent remember their heritage at the highland games in Batesville.

creationism as an alternative to evolution when explaining how humanity came into existence. This brought the biblical story of Adam and Eve into science classrooms all over the state. Although the law was later declared unconstitutional, the fact that it passed in the first place shows how strong Christian fundamentalism is in Arkansas.

Though Arkansans share many basic values, they express them

ETHNIC ARKANSAS

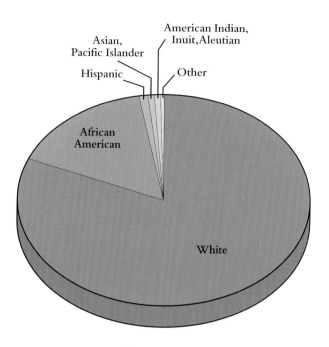

Asian, Pacific Islander

American Indian, Inuit, Aleutian

Hispanic

Other

African American

White

in different ways. Mountain ways are different from Delta ways, and Delta ways are different from western ways.

MOUNTAIN FOLK

In the knobs and hollers of the Ozarks, the old ways are still alive. People still practice folk crafts, such as whittling and quilting. They go hunting and berrying in the woods and use herbal lore to treat common illnesses. They dance to the music of fiddle, banjo, and mountain dulcimer (a stringed instrument that is plucked like a banjo and produces a vibrating, metallic sound). They sing with a "high lonesome" wail. Cooks still make the foods their forefathers enjoyed.

Many a modern Ozark family saves on the grocery bill with "poorboy suppers"—beans, corn bread, and "a mess of greens." Collard and turnip greens are the most popular type of greens. There's a knack to cooking them. Greens should be seasoned with salt and fatback (salt pork), then simmered until they look like a soggy green clump. "If your greens still look pretty, it's for sure and certain they haven't boiled long enough," said one experienced cook.

Other staples of Ozark cooking are pork, corn, and sorghum molasses. Arkansans eat many kinds of pork products, from break-

Arkansans are determined to keep their strong folk music tradition alive.

ARKANSAS CORN BREAD

Nothing says Arkansas better than a pan of fresh corn bread. This recipe is quick and easy.

1 cup cornmeal	1 teaspoon salt
1 cup unbleached flour	⅓ cup shortening
¼ cup sugar	1 egg
1 tablespoon baking powder	1 cup milk

What to do:

1. Measure cornmeal, flour, sugar, baking powder, and salt into a large bowl and mix them together.

2. In another bowl, mix shortening, egg, and milk.

3. Stir the shortening mixture into the dry ingredients. Mix just enough to blend it into a thick batter.

4. Rub an 8-inch square baking pan with butter.

5. Pour the batter into the pan.

6. Get an adult to help with the baking. Your corn bread should bake in a 400-degree oven for 25 minutes.

After it is done baking, cut the corn bread into squares. For a real Arkansas-style breakfast, butter a piece of hot corn bread and top with sorghum molasses.

fast sausages to sugar-cured hams. Corn can be served as a vegetable or made into meal for corn bread, cornmeal mush, and batters for coating fried vegetables and meats. The early settlers used molasses in place of sugar, which was expensive and hard to get. Modern cooks use molasses in recipes that need its special flavor.

Today, most people buy their molasses in the store. Only a few people still know how to make it by hand. The work is not only difficult and time consuming, but it needs a special touch. The maker must know when to pick the sorghum cane, how to operate the handpress that squeezes out the juice, and how to filter out impurities so the juice is ready for cooking. The molasses is cooked in flat copper pans over a hickory fire. Here, skill really comes into play; the cook must know how long to cook the syrup and how hot to make the fire. The best molasses is thick, sweet, and deep golden brown in color.

SPIRIT OF THE FRONTIER

Near its border with Oklahoma and Texas, Arkansas takes on the feel of the Old West. In these parts, people work as cattle ranchers and lumberjacks. Western dress is never out of fashion, rodeos are always a big draw, and a thick steak is considered the best eating around. Musicians are more likely to play electric guitars than mountain dulcimers. When they sing, a country-western twang replaces the high lonesome wail of the mountains.

In the old days, western Arkansas was a true frontier. It had everything—outlaws, saloon brawls, and an occasional shootout in

At the Ozark Folk Center, sorghum molasses is still made the old-fashioned way.

Everyone comes out for the Fort Smith Rodeo parade.

the streets of some dusty cow town. It even had a genuine "hangin' judge." Citizens of Fort Smith take great pride in remembering Judge Isaac Parker, who hanged eighty-eight criminals during his twenty-one years on the bench.

DELTA LIFE

On the Mississippi Delta, life moves with the rhythms of the river, and "southern hospitality" still matters. The people here are mainly farmers, working some of the richest soil in the country. Their work is seasonal, often backbreaking, and usually low paid.

The Delta is home to many African Americans, some of whom farm the land their ancestors worked as slaves. As black people in a white-dominated society, they still face many challenges. Racial segregation is no longer legal in Arkansas, but in practice it still exists in some places. Blacks and whites rarely live in the same neighborhoods, for example. White people control most local governments, police departments, and social service agencies.

Many families in the Delta face difficulties because of the region's limited job opportunities.

African-American culture has a strong base in religion. In black communities up and down the Delta, Sunday is a day for "preaching, praying, and praising," as one minister put it. Congregations that don't have a church of their own meet in storefronts or people's homes. If they don't have a preacher, a member of the congregation will offer up a few words. If they don't have someone who can play the piano, they sing unaccompanied.

Outside of church, the music of choice is the blues, with its strong beat and moody lyrics. The picturesque river town of

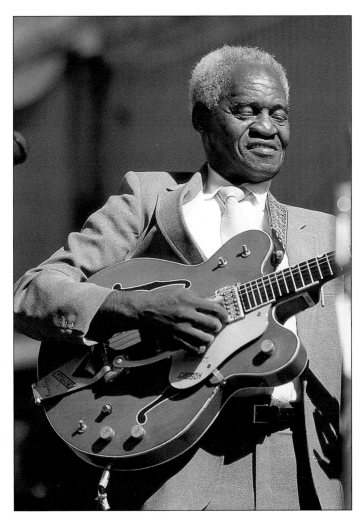

The blues is king in Helena.

Helena is noted for its blues clubs, smoky little places where black performers share their music with appreciative audiences. Helena is the home of the King Biscuit Time radio program, which has aired since November 1941. It has become a genuine Arkansas institution, still broadcasting the blues Mondays through Fridays to listeners throughout the region.

THE NEWCOMERS

While Arkansas is far from being a multicultural society, in recent years it has attracted immigrants from Asia and Latin America. Unlike African Americans who share language, religion, and many cultural traditions with the white majority, these newcomers often honor different traditions, speak different languages, and worship in different ways. Locals have had to stretch themselves to understand these new residents.

The Hmong, the Vietnamese, and other Southeast Asians fled war-torn homelands for a new life in America. Most are Buddhists and arrived in the United States speaking little or no English. Some settled in the Delta, finding work in rice fields much like those they left behind in Asia. Others went to the cities, bringing some of the sights and sounds of home to new neighborhoods in a new land.

In the 1990s, thousands of Latinos came into Arkansas from Central and South America, seeking economic opportunity. Their native tongue is Spanish, their religion, usually Catholic. The flourishing poultry industry drew many of them to the northwest corner of the state. More than 20,000 Latinos now live in the four-county area near the border of Missouri and Oklahoma.

Latino culture is beginning to make an impact on Arkansas communities. In July 1997, the town of Van Buren changed its annual Independence Day celebration into a multicultural festival. The planning committee printed flyers in Spanish and English. Food with a Latin flavor and music with a Latin beat joined the traditional hot dogs, watermelon, and Ozark folk music. Baptist kids from the Ozarks and Catholic kids from Mexico and El Salvador took turns swinging sticks to try to break open piñatas filled with candy. "We're in a global economy," one of the organizers told the *Arkansas Democrat-Gazette*. "It's time for people, right down to Van Buren, Arkansas, to understand other people's cultures."

LEGENDARY ARKANSAS

Arkansas folklore is a rich tradition, drawn from a people who seem to be natural storytellers. It is varied, colorful, and a great deal of fun. The tall tale, or windy, as Arkansans call it, is a specialty of the state. A good windy is based on exaggeration: the hero so strong he could whip his weight in wildcats; the weather so hot it made corn pop in the fields; the cabin so small you had to step outside to change your mind.

Sometimes the windy is a joke, and sometimes it's a game. The joke uses wild exaggeration to get a laugh. The game is more complicated—the teller spins a lengthy tale to see how far he or she can go before the listener realizes what's happening.

A popular relative of the windy is the "eyewitness" account of some outlandish creature. For example, the teller relates seeing a species of poisonous snake that bites its own tail, forming a hoop, and then proceeds to roll after its prey at fantastic speeds.

The "catywhompus" is an Ozark classic. It is a shaggy animal with two long legs on one side of its body and two short legs on the other. The catywhompus is built for racing around mountains. Unfortunately, it can only go in one direction, because the long legs must always be on the "down" side. On the flats, the poor thing can't budge.

Arkansas folklore is full of monstrous creatures, not all of them

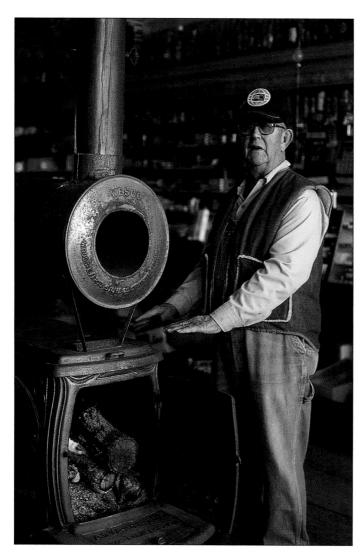

There are few better ways of whiling away the afternoon than at the general store.

THE GHOST TRAIN OF BOONE COUNTY

Up Boone County way, folks know a ghost when they see one, even if the ghost happens to be a train. You see, some years back, the Missouri and North Arkansas Railroad ran through there. Right from the start, that ole' M&NA gave passengers and station agents conniption fits.

Doggone thing was never on time. It passed up places it was supposed to stop, and stopped at places it was supposed to pass. When it finally got where it was going, all the passengers would be in a tizzy and half the baggage would be lost.

Folks took to calling the M&NA the old May-Never-Arrive. Long after the railroad shut down, hoboes camping under the trestle would see a caboose racing down the tracks in the moonlight. Dern thing never made a sound. It just rolled on for a spell, then up and disappeared.

Those hoboes thought they'd seen some devilish goings-on, but the local folks told 'em not to worry. It was just the ghost of the old May-Never-Arrive, bein' late to its own funeral.

as humorous as the catywhompus. Ozark folk had fun with the catywhompus, but nobody really believed that it existed. Many have believed in the White River monster. Off and on for more than a hundred years, people have reported seeing a monster in the river. It was as big as a boxcar, this monster, with a smooth gray hide and a knack for appearing just often enough to keep its legend alive.

Like the abominable snowman, the White River monster could never be captured or photographed. No one could say where it lived, or why it stayed in the river. It was a mystery, and Arkansans love a mystery, particularly if it has a hint of the monstrous.

In 1973, the state legislature decided to honor the legend—and have a little fun—by creating the White River Monster Sanctuary and Retreat. They carefully described the borders of this preserve and made a formal resolution that "no monster may be molested, killed or trampled" in the sanctuary.

FACING THE FUTURE

For most of its history, Arkansas has seemed like a cultural time capsule, populated by hardy, God-fearing folk who were generally happy with their lot in life. When the Little Rock Nine forced white Arkansans to face their own racism, new issues appeared. Arkansans grappled with those issues as best they could. For many, change was both slow and painful.

The creation of a broader and more tolerant society is an ongoing process. Many Arkansans are opening themselves to other cultures while protecting—and sharing—their own cherished values.

A group of young Arkansans enjoy the fine weather at Pinnacle Mountain State Park.

5 ARKANSAS STANDOUTS

Arkansas has produced standout achievers in many different fields, from professional sports to music, movies, and politics. Perhaps because Arkansas is a small state, people take a certain "family pride" in the achievements of homegrown celebrities.

THE BASKETBALL SUPERSTAR

In 1987, Scottie Pippen was the fifth player chosen in the National Basketball Association (NBA) draft. Ten years later, Pippen was a star for the Chicago Bulls. He had won two Olympic gold medals and five NBA championships and had been named one of the fifty greatest players in NBA history. The story of his rise to NBA stardom has become a classic of sorts.

That story began in the south Arkansas town of Hamburg. Pippen was born there on September 25, 1965, the youngest of twelve children of a paper mill worker. Scottie loved sports, especially basketball. "We'd play one-on-one forever," said his childhood friend Ron Martin. "We were convinced that one of us was going to make it to the NBA."

They were not convinced that the one to make it would be Scottie. By his senior year of high school, Pippen was a skinny, six-feet-one-inch-tall point guard who hadn't been recruited by any colleges. He went to the University of Central Arkansas on a grant,

Scottie Pippen goes in for a dunk.

to act as manager of the basketball team. He handed out towels, took care of equipment, and generally made himself useful to the coaches.

Between classes and locker room duties, he practiced with the team. He also grew. He soon cracked the starting lineup, and his managing duties were a thing of the past. By the end of his senior year, he was six feet seven and a prime NBA prospect.

He became the Chicago Bulls' "other guard," opposite megastar Michael Jordan. It was not an easy role to play. Jordan's winning charm and amazing skills made him the focus of media attention. The rest of the team became a supporting cast for the Michael Jordan Show. Pippen never seemed to resent his teammate's special status, or to want that kind of celebrity for himself. "I wouldn't ever want to be him," he once said. "To have to stay in the room all day long, because so many people are waiting outside? To always have the feeling that someone is standing behind you, listening, just recording everything you say? No. I don't know how he does it."

On the court, Pippen is awe-inspiring but not especially flashy. In endorsements and public appearances, he is understated and sometimes droll. He doesn't try for the breezy manner that comes so naturally to Michael Jordan. Off the court and out of the spotlight, his life is still his own.

THE ACADEMY AWARD WINNER

In 1981, Mary Steenburgen won the Best Supporting Actress Oscar for her role as the ditsy but strangely dignified Lynda Dummar in *Melvin and Howard*. It was the fulfillment of a lifelong dream for the young actress from North Little Rock.

Steenburgen was the eldest daughter of a railroad conductor and a school secretary. Her early life was normal enough, except that she always felt a gnawing concern about her father's health. Maurice Steenburgen suffered five heart attacks when Mary was young. The little girl tiptoed through her childhood, fearful of doing anything that might trigger another attack. She channeled her energies into make-believe and reading. "I know that's why I became an actress," Steenburgen once said. "In my dream world I could get mad and

Film critic Leonard Maltin once called Mary Steenburgen "one of the screen's most compulsively watchable actresses."

scream and yell, and if somebody died, they got up again. In real life, I didn't dare try it."

At nineteen, Mary Steenburgen packed up her clothes and her courage and headed for New York City. She studied acting while she worked as a waitress to pay the bills.

Five years later she was in Los Angeles, starring opposite actor-director Jack Nicholson in an offbeat Western called *Goin' South*. Nicholson had chosen the unknown young actress because she could be tough, determined, and even stubborn without losing her southern belle charm. With that, her movie career was off and running.

Today, Mary Steenburgen has a respected string of film credits behind her and the luxury of accepting parts only when she wants them. She still has that combination of toughness and refinement that caught Jack Nicholson's eye and launched her motion picture career.

THE POET

Maya Angelou is most often described as a poet, but many other words would work just as well: author, actress, singer, songwriter,

"All of my work, my life, everything is about survival," says Maya Angelou. "All my work is meant to say, 'You may encounter many defeats, but you must not be defeated.'"

MAYA ANGELOU REMEMBERS ARKANSAS

In *I Know Why the Caged Bird Sings*, Maya Angelou recalled her childhood in small-town Arkansas.

In Stamps the custom was to can everything that could possibly be preserved. During the killing season, after the first frost, all neighbors helped each other to slaughter hogs. . . . The missionary ladies of the Christian Methodist Episcopal Church helped Momma prepare the pork for sausage. They squeezed their fat arms deep in the ground meat, mixed it with gray nose-opening sage, pepper and salt, and made tasty little samples for all obedient children who brought wood for the slick black stove. The men chopped off the larger pieces of meat and laid them in the smokehouse to begin the curing process. . . . Throughout the year, until the next frost, we took our meals from the smokehouse, the little garden . . . and from the shelves of canned foods. There were choices on the shelves that could set a hungry child's mouth to watering. Green beans, snapped always the right length, collards, cabbage, juicy red tomato preserves that came into their own on steaming buttered biscuits, and sausage, beets, berries and every fruit grown in Arkansas.

film director, teacher, civil rights activist. She is all these and more.

Born in 1928, Angelou grew up in Stamps, near the corner of Arkansas that borders Texas and Louisiana. Her childhood was harsh. She was a black child in a strictly segregated white world, growing up in the middle of a terrible economic depression. Her

1970 book, *I Know Why the Caged Bird Sings*, is an honest, unsentimental account of her difficult childhood. It has become a modern American classic. For nearly thirty years, people have read it and wondered how this young girl endured a life that would have destroyed many people.

Angelou has published ten best-selling books, written songs that were recorded by blues legend B. B. King, and won a Tony Award for her performance in the Broadway drama *Look Away*. In 1977, she received an Emmy nomination for her acting in the television epic *Roots*.

In 1993, Angelou read an original poem at the inauguration of President Bill Clinton. The poem, "On the Pulse of Morning," was realistic about the past and hopeful about the future. In what might have been the most unusual tribute ever given to a poet, *Newsday* magazine made Angelou's reading available to everyone on a special toll-free phone line. Thousands of Americans dialed the number to hear the poem.

THE CRUSADING EDITOR

Not many people outside of Arkansas have heard of Harry Ashmore. But this Pulitzer Prize–winning editor of the *Arkansas Gazette* played an important role in the Little Rock school integration crisis of 1957. He risked his reputation and perhaps even his life to criticize Governor Orval Faubus for his racist stand.

Ashmore was born in South Carolina. As a product of the South, he understood the region's racial divisions. To some degree, he shared white prejudices, but he was able to separate personal

Arkansas Gazette *editor Harry*
Ashmore faced irate politicians and
canceled subscriptions when he argued
that white Arkansans needed to accept
integration and move into the future.

feelings from public policy. "Philosophically, we all knew segregation was wrong," he once told an interviewer.

When Governor Faubus called out the Arkansas National Guard
to stop the Little Rock Nine from entering Central High, Ashmore
spoke out. He called for moderation and accused Faubus of creating
the crisis for his own political ends.

Ashmore's stand drew death threats from extremists, advertising
boycotts from local merchants, and canceled subscriptions from
many *Gazette* readers. Through all of it, Ashmore stood his ground.
After Central High was finally integrated, Ashmore called upon the
people to accept the new order. American society was changing, he

said. In the name of liberty and justice, people were rethinking their attitudes about race. It was time for Arkansas to do the same.

The crisis ended, the nine African-American students entered Central High, and Harry Ashmore won the Pulitzer Prize. In 1959, he moved to California, but his interest in race relations that had been kindled by the standoff at Central High continued throughout his life, and he published several books on the topic. Harry Ashmore died on January 20, 1998, at the age of eighty-one.

THE MAN IN BLACK

Singer-songwriter Johnny Cash has been in the music industry for more than forty years. During that time, he has become a near-mythic figure—the rebel, the stranger, the outsider.

Cash was born in Kingsland, Arkansas, on February 26, 1932. His father farmed cotton until he lost his land and livelihood in the Great Depression. With the farm gone, the elder Cash did any sort of work he could find. Johnny grew up poor.

After a stint in the air force, Cash picked up the guitar he'd taught himself to play and moved to Memphis, Tennessee, where a promoter named Sam Phillips was recording the likes of Carl Perkins, Jerry Lee Lewis—and Elvis Presley.

Soon, the craggy-faced Cash had the first of his forty-eight hit singles. Over the course of his long career, he has sold more than 50 million albums. He has been inducted into both the Country Music and Rock and Roll Halls of Fame. His signature tunes, such as "I Walk the Line" and "Fulsom Prison Blues," are classics. His signature costume is equally well known.

"Hello, I'm Johnny Cash," says the music legend at the beginning of each concert.

There are several stories about how Johnny Cash became the Man in Black. Some believe he began wearing black as a social statement. Many trace it back to his 1971 anti–Vietnam War song, "Man in Black." Cash himself gives a more down-to-earth reason. When he first started playing, wearing black saved the expense of matching wardrobes for himself and his musicians. He stuck with it because it felt comfortable onstage. Today, it's just the way of things; Cash's fans expect it.

THE PRESIDENT

Bill Clinton overcame tremendous odds to become the first U.S. president from Arkansas. He wasn't exactly born in a log cabin like Abraham Lincoln, but he did come from modest circumstances. William Jefferson Blythe IV was born on August 19, 1946, in Hope, Arkansas. His mother was Virginia Cassidy Blythe. His father, William Jefferson Blythe III, had been killed in a car accident three months earlier.

In 1950, the young widow married Roger Clinton, a car dealer. Three years later, the family moved from Hope to Hot Springs, where Bill's half brother, Roger, was born. It wasn't an easy life, or an especially happy one. Bill's stepfather was an alcoholic with a temper, and he had little patience with children.

Bill threw himself into school and music. By the time he graduated from high school in 1964, he played a fine tenor saxophone and had discovered a knack for leadership through his involvement in school clubs and activities.

He went to Georgetown University in Washington, D.C., where his outstanding performance earned him a Rhodes scholarship to study at England's famed Oxford University. After two years at Oxford, he returned to the United States, where he entered law school at Yale University. After he graduated from Yale in 1973, Clinton took a teaching job at the University of Arkansas Law School in Fayetteville. But teaching wouldn't hold him for long.

The call of politics was already shaping Clinton's life when he married fellow Yale alumna Hillary Rodham in 1975. In 1978, he became the youngest governor in Arkansas history. He was thirty-

Young Bill Clinton sits atop a pony in Hope.

Bill Clinton is famous for his ability to relate to ordinary people.

two, ambitious, and self-assured. Clinton served five terms as governor and became increasingly active on the national political scene.

In 1991, he began campaigning for the presidency. The field was full of Democratic hopefuls, vying for the chance to run against President George Bush. Bill Clinton was a masterful campaigner. He toured the country by bus, meeting people on their own terms. He talked politics, but he also reached out on other levels. For example, he donned designer sunglasses to play a saxophone solo on national television. The president can be approachable, Bill Clinton seemed to be saying. He can be human. Clinton defeated Bush, and in 1996, he won a second term.

Though Arkansas has given the nation a president, it is still not known for setting trends or for being on the leading edge of social change. This does not mean it hasn't produced its fair share of achievers, exceptional people in many walks of life, who have given the home folks reason to be proud.

6 THE GRAND TOUR

Lake Enterprise

With its rich history, colorful folklore, and many natural wonders, Arkansas has a wealth of interesting sights. Let's take an imaginary tour of some of them.

THE DELTA

We'll start where the first European settlers started in 1686, at Arkansas Post, near where the Arkansas River meets the Mississippi. It was here that Henri de Tonti and his party decided to make a home in the New World.

Today, the place where pioneers first got a foothold in the future state of Arkansas is a national memorial. Nearby, a museum houses artifacts and documents tracing Arkansas history back to colonial times.

Moving northward along the Great River Road, which runs alongside the Mississippi, we come to Helena, Arkansas's home of the blues. A restored railroad depot from 1912 houses the Delta Cultural Center, which offers exhibits and educational programs about the history and culture of the region. A featured attraction is a music exhibit that begins with the earliest blues and goes through the rockabilly sound of the 1950s. Another popular spot is Sonny Boy's Music Hall, a picturesque café that features live blues performances.

PLACES TO SEE

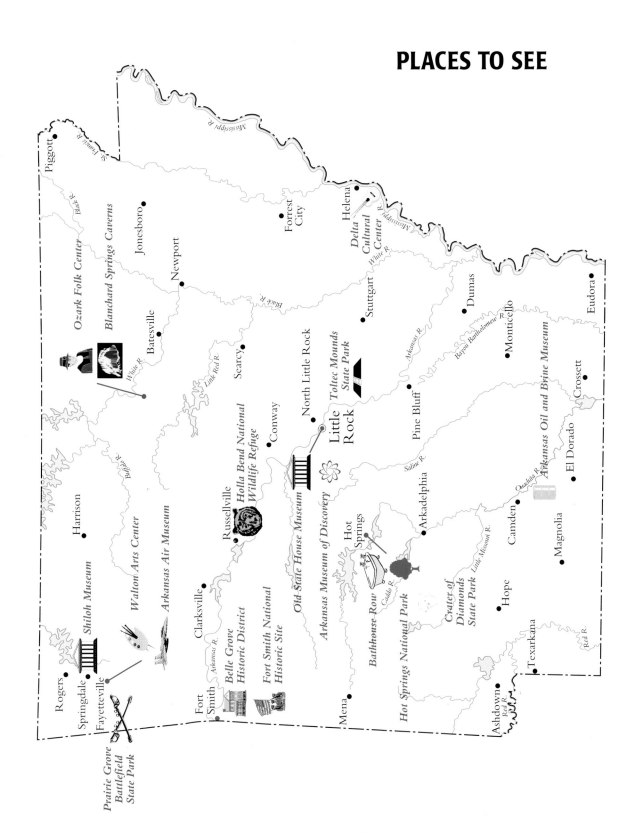

Piggott

Mississippi R.

St. Francis R.

Black R.

Ozark Folk Center

Blanchard Springs Caverns

Jonesboro

Forrest City

Helena

Delta Cultural Center

Mississippi R.

Newport

Black R.

White R.

Stuttgart

Dumas

Eudora

Batesville

White R.

Little Red R.

Searcy

North Little Rock

Toltec Mounds State Park

Arkansas R.

Bayou Bartholomew R.

Monticello

Arkansas Oil and Brine Museum

Crossett

Conway

Little Rock

Pine Bluff

El Dorado

Harrison

Buffalo R.

Walton Arts Center

Arkansas Air Museum

Russellville

Holla Bend National Wildlife Refuge

Old State House Museum

Arkansas Museum of Discovery

Saline R.

Arkadelphia

Ouachita R.

Camden

Magnolia

Shiloh Museum

Clarksville

Arkansas R.

Belle Grove Historic District

Fort Smith National Historic Site

Hot Springs

Bathhouse Row

Caddo R.

Crater of Diamonds State Park

Little Missouri R.

Hope

Rogers

Springdale

Fayetteville

Fort Smith

Mena

Hot Springs National Park

Texarkana

Red R.

Prairie Grove Battlefield State Park

Ashdown

Red R.

THE FASTEST FESTIVAL IN ARKANSAS

Lake Chicot is a genuine Arkansas landmark, the largest natural oxbow lake in North America.

The lake is the perfect setting for the annual U.S. Title Series Hydroplane Races. The race is the featured attraction of the annual Lake Chicot Water Festival. Every year in late June, speedboaters descend on the quiet little town of Lake Village.

For those who don't care for boat racing, there's plenty more to see: an acrobatic air show, daredevil bike and skateboard exhibitions, and a fireworks display. People who enjoy quieter pursuits can explore arts and crafts displays, listen to the music of nationally known bands, or attend the always hilarious "beauty pageant" to choose Mr. Lake Chicot.

THE OZARKS

Moving westward from the Delta, we arrive at Powhatan, which has a striking brick courthouse with delicate woodwork. The building was constructed in 1888 and served as the seat of Lawrence County government for almost a hundred years. It is now a museum, with displays that reflect life in the eastern Ozarks. In addition to the courthouse, a county jail from 1873 and a pre–Civil War log house have also been restored.

Ozark Folk Center State Park in Mountain View is a living museum. It recreates the folk culture of the mountains: artisans demonstrate pioneer skills, and musicians perform on old-time folk instruments. The center is both a tourist attraction and a place that preserves a way of life that might otherwise be lost.

Northward near the Missouri line, the Top o' the Ozarks Tower juts skyward from the summit of Bull Mountain. It stands 140 feet tall and is equipped with an elevator for easy access. The structure was built as a lookout, carefully placed to offer the best view of the White River valley below.

Nearby, Mountain Village 1890 is a settlement from the last century. Visiting the little community, with its authentic buildings and costumed actors, is like stepping through a time warp. Nearby, the Bull Shoals Caverns create their own time-warp effect. In these underground chambers prehistoric humans found homes, Civil War soldiers found shelter, and moonshiners found a place to hide their illegal whiskey.

Farther west in Eureka Springs, the seven-story Christ of the Ozarks statue overlooks a museum, a memorial chapel, and an

Touring Mountain Village 1890, with its old-fashioned shops and buggies, is like stepping back in time.

Point Bluff provides a spectacular view of the Ozarks.

*Spinning wool at the Ozark
Folk Center*

The Christ of the Ozarks statue looms seven stories over Eureka Springs.

amphitheater. The statue depicts Jesus with arms extended straight out from the shoulders, making the figure itself resemble a cross.

In Fayetteville, the Walton Arts Center is an impressive complex with theaters, art galleries, rehearsal studios, and more. The center is home to the North Arkansas Symphony and frequent host to Broadway touring shows.

On the edge of town, the Arkansas Air Museum at Drake Field

preserves vintage aircraft, including pre–World War II racing planes that have been restored to flying condition. The museum is head-quartered in a historic hangar that dates back to the days when aviation was in its infancy and pilots barnstormed around the country, giving exhibitions and rides.

THE WEST AND THE HEARTLAND

Many Fort Smith landmarks reflect the city's frontier past. Down-town, the Belle Grove Historic District is a source of pride. It is a twenty-two-block area of restored homes, many of them more than a hundred years old.

At the Fort Smith National Historic Site, the courtroom of "Hangin' Judge" Isaac Parker is carefully preserved, along with the jail where criminals awaited their appointment with justice. There is also a reproduction of the gallows where many of those criminals met their end.

The neighboring town of Van Buren has transformed its down-town area into what looks like a nineteenth-century shopping district. The people who work in the art galleries, antique shops, and restaurants dress to match the setting. So do some of the tourists who come for a taste of the past. The atmosphere is so authentic that Van Buren's historic downtown has often been used for film locations.

Little Rock, in central Arkansas, is the largest city in the state. As the state capital, it has many impressive public buildings. Two of the most notable are the former and present capitol buildings. Construction of the Old State House was begun in 1833 and was

Eighty-eight men died at the Fort Smith gallows after trials presided over by "Hangin' Judge" Isaac Parker. "It was not I who hung them," Parker said. "It was the law."

finished in 1842. Its Greek Revival style, with graceful columns and clean, classic lines, was popular for public buildings of the time. Today, the Old State House is a museum, featuring displays such as political memorabilia, African-American quilts, and the inaugural ball gowns of Arkansas's first ladies.

The present statehouse is modeled on the nation's Capitol in Washington, D.C. Construction began in 1899, but it was 1911 before the legislature could meet in its impressive new chambers. The capitol complex includes a Vietnam memorial, the Liberty Bell Pavilion, and beautifully landscaped gardens that lend an air of southern graciousness to the nitty-gritty business of politics.

THE SOUTHWEST

Moving south into the Ouachitas, we come to a town that is an Arkansas landmark all by itself: Hot Springs, home of the famous mineral waters and a renowned artists colony.

At the very heart of Hot Springs is Bathhouse Row, named a national historic landmark in 1987. Bathhouse Row consists of

Pinnacle Mountain State Park outside of Little Rock is devoted to teaching Arkansans about preserving the environment.

The crashing Cossatot River in the Ouachita Mountains has been called "the most difficult whitewater stream in the state of Arkansas."

eight bathhouses built in the early twentieth century. At that time, health consciousness was the latest fad, and people believed that "taking the waters" at mineral hot springs could cure whatever ailed them. Today, only one of the eight is still a functioning bathhouse. Another serves as a visitor center and museum.

The Hot Springs Mountain Tower is a 216-foot observation post atop Hot Springs Mountain. Two viewing levels offer stunning views of Hot Springs National Park and the Ouachita Mountains.

Moving southward into the rolling timberlands, we come to the nineteenth-century town of Washington. The town was established in 1824 and became a regular stop for Texas-bound pioneers. Davy Crockett stopped there. So did Sam Houston and James Bowie. From 1863 to 1865, Washington served as the Confederate capital of Arkansas. The capitol building has been restored, along with a tavern, various shops, and several residences.

Closer to the Louisiana border, near the small town of Smackover, three oil derricks mark the Arkansas Museum of Natural Resources. The museum features a working oil well and pumping rig as well as the three derricks. Inside, exhibits include artifacts and video presentations detailing the history of the 1920s oil boom in southern Arkansas.

Texarkana, the city that straddles two states (Arkansas and Texas) and is named for three (Texas, Arkansas, and Louisiana), makes a good ending point for our tour of Arkansas. One of its most popular landmarks is Photographer's Island on State Line Avenue. Here, generations of tourists have posed for snapshots with one foot in Arkansas and the other in Texas. Somehow, this seems fitting in a state that is part Wild West, part Old South, and part hill country.

THE FLAG: Adopted in 1913, the flag is a white diamond on a red field. The 25 stars around the diamond indicate that Arkansas was the 25th state to join the Union. The four stars in the center represent Spain, France, the United States, and the Confederate States of America, the four governments that have ruled Arkansas.

THE SEAL: In the seal's center is a shield in front of an American eagle. The shield displays wheat, a steamboat, a beehive, and a plow, which symbolize agricultural and industrial wealth. Above the eagle is the Goddess of Liberty and to the sides are the Angel of Mercy and the Sword of Justice. The seal was adopted in 1907.

STATE SURVEY

Statehood: June 15, 1836

Origin of Name: From *acansa*, meaning "south wind," a Sioux Indian term for the Quapaws

Nickname: Land of Opportunity

Capital: Little Rock

Motto: The People Rule

Bird: Mockingbird

Flower: Apple blossom

Tree: Pine

Insect: Honeybee

Gem: Diamond

Mockingbird

Apple blossom

ARKANSAS (STATE SONG)

"Arkansas" was adopted as the official state song in 1917. It was replaced, then readopted in 1963.

Words and Music by
Eva Ware Barnett

I am think-ing to-night of the South-land, Of the home of my child-hood days, Where I roamed thro' the woods and the mea-dows, By the mill and the brook that plays; Where the ros-es are in bloom, And the sweet mag-no-lia too, Where the jas-mine is white, And the fields are vio-let blue. There a wel-come a-waits all her chil-dren Who have wan-dered so far from home. Ark-an-sas, Ark-an-sas, 'Tis a name dear. 'Tis the place I call "Home, Sweet Home." Ark-an-sas, Ark-an-sas, I sa-lute thee, From thy shel-ter no more I'll roam,

GEOGRAPHY

Highest Point: 2,753 feet above sea level, at Magazine Mountain

Lowest Point: 55 feet, at the Ouachita River in Ashley and Union Counties

Area: 53,183 square miles

Greatest Distance, North to South: 240 miles

Greatest Distance, East to West: 276 miles

Bordering States: Oklahoma and Texas to the west, Missouri to the north, Tennessee and Mississippi to the east, and Louisiana to the south

Hottest Recorded Temperature: 120° F in Ozark on August 10, 1936

Coldest Recorded Temperature: -29° F in Benton County on February 13, 1905

Average Annual Precipitation: 49 inches

Major Rivers: Arkansas, Black, Mississippi, Ouachita, Red, St. Francis, White

Major Lakes: Beaver, Bull Shoals, Catherine, Chicot, Dardanelle, Felsenthal, Millwood, Norfolk, Ouachita

Trees: ash, basswood, buckeye, dogwood, elm, hickory, holly, locust, maple, oak, pine

Wild Plants: azalea, bluebell, hydrangea, lady's slipper, passionflower, water lily, wild verbena, yellow jasmine

Animals: black bear, bobcat, mink, muskrat, opossum, raccoon, razorback hog, skunk, weasel, white-tailed deer, woodchuck

Birds: brown thrasher, cardinal, duck, goldfinch, goose, mockingbird, pheasant, phoebe, quail, robin, whippoorwill, wild turkey

Fish: bass, bream, catfish, crappie, perch, pickerel, sturgeon, trout

Endangered Animals: American burying beetle, American peregrine falcon, Arkansas fatmucket, bald eagle, cave crayfish, Curtis' pearlymussel, fat pocketbook, gray bat, Indiana bat, least tern, leopard darter, Magazine Mountain shagreen, Ouachita rock-pocketbook, Ozark big-eared bat, Ozark cavefish, pallid sturgeon, pink mucket pearlymussel, red-cockaded woodpecker, speckled pocketbook

Endangered Plants: eastern prairie fringed orchid, harperella, pond-berry, running buffalo clover

Eastern prairie fringed orchid

TIMELINE

Arkansas History

1500s Caddo, Osage, and Quapaw Indians inhabit the region

1541 Hernando de Soto is the first European to explore the region

1682 René-Robert Cavelier, Sieur de La Salle, claims the region for France

1686 The first European settlement in present-day Arkansas is established in what would become Arkansas Post

1803 Arkansas becomes U.S. territory as part of the Louisiana Purchase

1819 Arkansas Territory is established with Arkansas Post as its capital; the *Arkansas Gazette*, the state's first newspaper, is established

1821 The capital moves to Little Rock

1836 Arkansas becomes the 25th state

1843 The state legislature establishes a public school system

1861 The Civil War begins; Arkansas secedes from the Union

1868 Arkansas is readmitted to the Union

1871 Arkansas Industrial University, later renamed the University of Arkansas, is founded in Fayetteville

1874 The present state constitution is adopted

1887 Bauxite is discovered near Little Rock

1888 The state's first free public library is established in Helena

1906 Diamonds are discovered near Murfreesboro

1921 Oil is discovered near El Dorado

1932 Arkansan Hattie Caraway becomes the first woman elected to the U.S. Senate

1957 Federal troops are sent in to help integrate Central High School in Little Rock

1967 Winthrop Rockefeller becomes the first Republican governor of Arkansas since 1874

1970 The McClellan-Kerr Arkansas River Navigation System is completed, allowing large boats to travel all the way across Arkansas to the Mississippi River

1992 Arkansan Bill Clinton is elected president

1996 Governor Jim Guy Tucker resigns after being convicted of conspiring to defraud financial institutions

ECONOMY

Agricultural Products: beef cattle, catfish, chickens, cotton, eggs, hogs, rice, soybeans, tomatoes, wheat

Manufactured Products: airplane parts, chemicals, clothing, electrical equipment, food products, furniture, lumber, paper, steel

Egg farm

Natural Resources: bauxite, bromine, cement, clay, natural gas, oil, sand and gravel, stone, timber

Business and Trade: medical services, tourism, transportation, wholesale and retail trade

CALENDAR OF CELEBRATIONS

Eagle Awareness Weekend Each January outdoor lovers gather in Lakeview to celebrate the bald eagle and other winter wildlife of the Ozarks. Highlights include barge tours to view eagles, guided bird walks, and owl prowls. You can also enjoy listening to guest speakers and live music.

Jonquil Festival This March festival celebrates the blooming of the jonquils that were planted by some of Hope's earliest settlers. Besides enjoying the fragrance of these lovely flowers, you can hear foot-stomping bluegrass music and watch demonstrations of traditional crafts.

Annual Dulcimer Jamboree The haunting sounds of the dulcimer drift through Mountain View during this April event. Musicians come from across the country to participate in workshops and contests. You can also hear performances by previous winners and admire traditional crafts.

Greek Food Festival At this May event in Little Rock, you can feast on luscious Greek and Middle Eastern food, watch Greek dancers, and attend a fashion show.

Riverfest Little Rock bursts to life each May with this celebration of the arts. The festival features ballet, theater, art exhibits, and musical performances to suit every taste. A bike race and a big fireworks display add to the fun.

Pink Tomato Festival The highlight of this June event in Warren is an all-tomato luncheon. The menu includes tomato juice, tomato cake, and carrots marinated in tomato soup. The festival also includes a tomato-eating contest, a parade of horse-drawn wagons, a street dance, and a cutest baby contest.

Rodeo of the Ozarks In July, Springdale hosts one of the nation's largest outdoor rodeos. At this celebration of cowboy skills, you can see all the traditional events, including bronco riding and calf roping.

Hope Watermelon Festival Watermelons grow to gigantic proportions in Hope—sometimes over 200 pounds. Each August Hope celebrates this with a festival featuring watermelon decorating, eating, and seed-spitting contests. In case visitors get tired of eating watermelon, there's also dancing, music, games, and a big fish fry.

Hope Watermelon Festival

Ozark Folk Festival Eureka Springs is home to the oldest folk festival west of the Mississippi. For three days each September, the town bursts with all kinds of folk music. There's also an arts and crafts show that brings the traditions of the Ozarks alive.

Autumnfest Each October Fayetteville celebrates the coming of autumn and the fall colors. You can watch parades, dance at the Harvest Ball, or just enjoy lots of delicious food and fun music.

Little Rock Air Force Base Open House Thousands of people visit the air force base in Jacksonville during this October open house to tour airplanes and watch a thrilling air show.

King Biscuit Blues Festival One of the largest festivals in the South, this celebration in Helena attracts blues fans from around the world each

October. Besides listening to great blues and gospel, visitors can stroll among antiques and crafts booths, play games, and eat lots of food.

Arkansas Rice Festival Each October Weiner celebrates Arkansas's place as the leading rice-producing state. At this festival, you can sample hundreds of rice dishes. Other activities include a cook-off and demonstrations of rice-harvesting machinery.

Wings over the Prairie Festival November is duck season in Stuttgart, and each year tens of thousands of people show up to watch competitors demonstrate their best duck calls. Besides all the quacking, the festival also features the crowning of Queen Mallard, a dance, an arts and crafts fair, and a duck gumbo cook-off.

Prairie Grove Battle Reenactment Every other year during the first weekend in December at Prairie Grove Battlefield State Park outside Fayetteville, costumed history buffs reenact this Civil War battle. The event also features a presentation on the life of a Civil War–era soldier.

STATE STARS

Maya Angelou (1928–   ), an African-American poet, actress, and singer, was born in St. Louis, Missouri, but moved to Stamps, Arkansas, when she was three years old. She is best known for her powerful story of her harsh childhood, *I Know Why the Caged Bird Sings*. Other well known works include *Just Give Me a Drink of Water Fore I Diiie* and *All God's Children Need Traveling Shoes*. As an actress, Angelou earned a Tony Award for her role in *Look Away* and an Emmy nomination for her part in the television miniseries *Roots*.

Daisy Bates

Daisy Bates (1920–   ), a civil rights activist, was born in Huttig. In 1941 she and her husband began publishing a newspaper called the *Arkansas State Press*, which attracted many readers by reporting incidents of mistreatment of blacks that were ignored in other papers. Bates eventually began working with the National Association for the Advancement of Colored People. She became a renowned civil rights leader when she headed the effort to desegregate the Little Rock public schools in 1957.

James Bridges (1936–1993), who was born in Paris, Arkansas, was a film director and screenwriter. Bridges originally set out to be an actor, but after a spell of winning nothing but bit parts, he turned his attention to writing and directing. He became well respected for making highly entertaining films that also have a strong social commentary. Bridges is best remembered for his films *The Paper Chase* and *The China Syndrome*.

Lou Brock (1939–   ) is considered one of the greatest base stealers in baseball history. Brock began his career with the Chicago Cubs. He transferred to the St. Louis Cardinals in 1964, sparking their World Series victory that year. For many years, he held the record for the number of career bases stolen—938. Brock, who was born in El Dorado, was inducted into the National Baseball Hall of Fame in 1985.

Dee Brown (1908–   ) is a historian who wrote *Bury My Heart at Wounded Knee*. This best-selling book discusses, from the Indian point of view, the slaughter of Native Americans and the destruction of their culture by the U.S. government in the 19th century. Brown was born in Louisiana and moved to Stephens, Arkansas, at age five. He attended Arkansas State Teachers College and eventually became a librarian and professor at the University of Illinois. Brown has written more than 20 books, including *American Spa*, a history of Hot Springs. After retiring from teaching in 1972, Brown returned to Arkansas to live.

Helen Gurley Brown (1922–   ) was editor in chief of *Cosmopolitan* magazine from 1966 until 1997. When she took over *Cosmopolitan*, the failing magazine was aimed at housewives. She immediately changed its focus in order to attract what became known as "Cosmo girls": smart, good-looking, hardworking single women. Brown added lots of material about relationships and emotions and eliminated material about cooking and raising children. By the time she was done, she had transformed *Cosmopolitan* into the remarkably successful "Bible of the Unmarried Woman." Brown was born in Green Forest and was raised in Little Rock.

Helen Gurley Brown

Paul "Bear" Bryant (1913–1983) won more games than any other college football coach in history. Born in Moro Bottoms and raised in Fordyce, Bryant earned his nickname when, as a youth, he wrestled a bear. He played college football, became an assistant coach right after graduation, and landed his first head-coaching

Paul "Bear" Bryant

assignment at the University of Maryland in 1945. He eventually became head coach at the University of Alabama in 1958 and remained there until he retired in 1982. By that time, he had chalked up 323 victories and 6 national championships.

Sarah Caldwell (1924–   ) is a renowned opera conductor who was raised in Fayetteville. A gifted child, Caldwell was giving violin recitals before age 10 and graduated from high school at 14. She founded the Opera Company of Boston in 1958 and brought it to national prominence, earning respect for her imaginative productions. In 1976, Caldwell became the first woman to conduct at New York's Metropolitan Opera.

Glen Campbell (1938–   ), who was born in Delight, is a popular country singer and songwriter. His best-known songs include "By the Time I Get to Phoenix," "Wichita Lineman," and "Rhinestone Cowboy." Campbell hosted his own television variety show in the 1970s.

Hattie Caraway (1878–1950), the first woman ever elected to the U.S. Senate, grew up in Tennessee. She met Thaddeus Caraway in college, and they soon married and settled in Jonesboro, Arkansas. Her husband eventually became a U.S. senator. After he died in 1931, she was appointed to complete his term. The following year, she ran for the seat herself and won.

During her career, she also became the first woman to preside over a session of the Senate, the first woman Senate committee chairperson, and the first woman to conduct a Senate committee hearing. Caraway served in the Senate until 1945.

Hattie Caraway

Johnny Cash (1932–   ), whose deep growl of a voice is known world-wide, is a giant in country music. Cash grew up in the dirt-poor town of Kingsland. In the 1950s, he taught himself to play guitar, moved to Memphis, Tennessee, and began performing and recording country and rockabilly songs. Many of his hits from this era, including "I Walk the Line" and "Fulsom Prison Blues," have become classics. Cash has been inducted into both the Rock and Roll and Country Music Halls of Fame.

Bill Clinton (1946–   ), the 42nd president of the United States, was born in Hope and grew up in Hot Springs. An excellent student, Clinton became a lawyer and began teaching law at the University of Arkansas. He soon became Arkansas's attorney general and, in 1978, was elected the youngest governor in the state's history. He served four more terms as governor, before being elected president in 1992. Clinton was reelected in 1996.

Dizzy Dean

Dizzy Dean (1911–1974), who was born in Lucas, was a legendary baseball pitcher. Dean took the major leagues by storm in 1932, his first full season, winning 18 games. Two years later, he won 30 games—a record that would stand for 34 years—and led the St. Louis Cardinals to a World Series victory. Before his career was cut short by injury, Dean had won 150 games. He was elected to the National Baseball Hall of Fame in 1953.

J. William Fulbright (1905–1995), a U.S. senator, was the force behind the prestigious Fulbright fellowships program. Fulbright grew up in Fayetteville, attended the University of Arkansas, and in 1943, began

J. William Fulbright

serving in the U.S. House of Representatives. He soon moved to the Senate, where he earned a reputation as a champion of international under-standing. His greatest legacy is the Fulbright program, which provides grants for American scholars to do research abroad and for foreign students to study in the U.S. Fulbright is also remembered because, in 1966, he became the first prominent member of Congress to criticize the Vietnam War.

Ellen Gilchrist (1935–), who lives in Fayetteville, is a well-respected poet and fiction writer. In such books as *In the Land of Dreamy Dreams* and *Falling through Space*, she has provided a candid view of well-to-do southern society. Her 1984 short story collection, *Victory over Japan*, won the American Book Award.

Al Green (1946–) is a popular soul and gospel singer from Forrest City. Green first hit number one in 1972, with "Let's Stay Together." After a string of hits in the 1970s, Green quit pop music to become a minister and a gospel singer. Green's smooth, silky voice has brought him critical acclaim—he's won nine Grammy Awards—and made him one of the most successful recording artists of all time.

Al Green

John Grisham (1955–) is a lawyer who has written a string of best-selling novels about the legal profes-sion. Many of his books, such as *The Firm*, *The Pelican Brief*, and *The Client*, have been made into popular movies. Grisham was born in Jonesboro.

John H. Johnson

John H. Johnson (1918–   ) is the head of the most powerful black publishing company in the United States. In 1942, he founded *Negro Digest*, a magazine that compiled articles of interest to African Americans from other newspapers and magazines. After *Negro Digest* quickly attracted a large readership, Johnson also founded *Ebony* and *Jet* magazines. Johnson was born in Arkansas City.

Scott Joplin (1868–1917), an African-American composer from Texarkana, was known as the King of Ragtime. Joplin popularized ragtime music, which was noted for its strong rhythms and lively, intricate melodies. His "Maple Leaf Rag" was the most popular ragtime song at the turn of the century—millions of copies of the sheet music were sold. Today, Joplin is best known for his song "The Entertainer," which earned wide popularity after it was used in the 1973 movie *The Sting*.

Alan Ladd (1913–1964) was a popular actor of the 1940s and 1950s. Ladd, who was born in Hot Springs, began his career performing small roles in movies and plays. His big break came when he was cast in the starring role as a paid killer in *This Gun for Hire*. From then on he appeared in film after film, playing quiet tough guys. His most famous role was as the mysterious stranger in the classic Western *Shane*.

Douglas MacArthur (1880–1964), one of the most celebrated soldiers of the 20th century, was born in Little Rock. He attended the United States Military Academy at West Point, where he graduated first in his class, and

Douglas MacArthur

then worked his was up through the army ranks to become a five-star general. During World War II, MacArthur became the supreme commander of Allied forces in the Pacific. He led United Nations forces during the Korean War until a conflict with President Harry Truman over whether to extend the war into China led to his dismissal.

Patsy Montana (1914–1996) of Hot Springs was the first major female star in country music. With her cowgirl image and her fantastic yodeling, she shot up the charts in 1935 with her hit "I Want to Be a Cowboy's Sweetheart." This was the first single by a female country singer to sell more than a million copies.

Patsy Montana

Scottie Pippen (1965–   ) has been a starting guard with the Chicago Bulls basketball team that has won the National Basketball Association (NBA) championship six times. Pippen was born in Hamburg and played college ball at the University of Central Arkansas. Pippen entered the pros in 1987, became a starter for the Bulls in 1988, and has been an all-star every year since 1990. In 1996, the NBA named Pippen one of the 50 greatest players of all time.

Brooks Robinson (1937–   ), a Little Rock native, is considered by many to be the greatest third baseman in the history of baseball. Robinson began playing for the Baltimore Orioles in 1955, and his outstanding fielding soon earned him acclaim. During his 22 years with the Orioles, his consistent defensive work earned him 16 Golden Glove Awards, more than anyone else has ever won. Robinson was elected to the National Baseball Hall of Fame in 1983.

Mary Steenburgen (1953–   ) is an Academy Award–winning actress from North Little Rock. Steenburgen made her movie debut opposite Jack Nicholson in the 1978 film *Goin' South*. Starring in such films as *Ragtime*, *Time and Again*, and *Parenthood*, she quickly established a reputation for playing characters that are soft-spoken, a bit eccentric, and often very determined. In 1981, she won the Best Supporting Actress Oscar for her role in *Melvin and Howard*.

William Grant Still (1895–1978) was a groundbreaking violinist and composer. Still was born in Mississippi and grew up in Little Rock. He played violin as a child but did not seriously consider music as a career until college. He eventually moved to New York City, where he began incorporating jazz and folk tunes into his compositions. In 1931, his *Afro-American Symphony* became the first symphony by a black American to be performed by a major orchestra. Still was also the first African American to conduct a major symphony orchestra and to have an opera performed by a major company.

William Grant Still

Barry Switzer (1937–   ), who was born in Crossett, is the head coach of the Dallas Cowboys football team. Switzer played college football at the University of Arkansas and later gained fame coaching at the University of Oklahoma, where he led his team to three national championships.

In 1994, Switzer became the head coach at Dallas. The following year he guided the Cowboys to a Super Bowl championship.

Sam Walton (1918–1992), who founded the Wal-Mart chain of stores, was for many years the richest man in the United States. Walton grew up in Missouri and began working in discount stores after college. Most discount chains had stores only in cities. Walton believed they were ignoring the huge market of smaller towns and suburbs. So in 1962 in Rogers, Arkansas, he opened the first Wal-Mart. His idea quickly took off. By the time he died, more than 1,700 Wal-Marts were spread across the country.

TOUR THE STATE

Arkansas Territorial Restoration (Little Rock) Four restored homes from the early 19th century give visitors a taste of frontier life.

Old State House Museum (Little Rock) The Old State House, built in 1836, is now a historical museum, where you can visit the restored legislative meeting rooms and governor's office. Another room is filled with hands-on exhibits, such as old clothes that can be tried on and tools of everyday life you can handle.

Arkansas Museum of Discovery (Little Rock) At this wide-ranging museum, you can build a robot, experiment with magnets, and construct a teepee.

Toltec Mounds Archaeological State Park (England) This was once the site of one of the largest Native American settlements in the region. Today, you can see the remnants of some of the mounds that were built between A.D. 700 and 950.

Blanchard Springs Caverns

Blanchard Springs Caverns (Mountain View) A tour of these spectacular caverns takes you past extraordinary cave formations and along a glistening cave stream.

Ozark Folk Center (Mountain View) This center is dedicated to preserving traditional Ozark culture. A highlight is watching craftspeople use traditional methods to make candles, pottery, and baskets. Performances of mountain music make a visit to the center all the more enjoyable.

Holla Bend National Wildlife Refuge (Dardanelle) Bald eagles, herons, egrets, sandpipers, ducks, and geese all make this wildlife refuge their winter home.

Crater of Diamonds State Park (Murfreesboro) The only place in North America where diamonds have been uncovered is now a park where you can hunt for them. Visitors have found about 70,000 so far.

Eureka Springs (Eureka Springs) This quaint 19th-century town is tucked into a mountainside. Droves of visitors come to wander the narrow streets and browse in the charming shops.

Arkansas Air Museum (Fayetteville) Housed in an old wooden hangar, this museum features antique airplanes and exhibits about the history of aviation.

Hot Springs National Park (Hot Springs) At this popular resort area, water comes up out of the ground at 143 degrees Fahrenheit. The park is home to several historic bathhouses that were built in the early 20th century, when people came to Hot Springs because they thought its water had healing powers. Today, in addition to taking to the waters, visitors can hike and make a trip up the Hot Springs Mountain Tower, which offers a spectacular view of the Ouachita Mountains.

Fort Smith National Historic Site (Fort Smith) One of the first U.S. military posts in the Louisiana Territory, this site offers a taste of the Old West. You can tour the courtroom where Judge Isaac Parker, the Hangin' Judge, presided and the jail in which prisoners were held.

Shiloh Museum (Springdale) This excellent museum is devoted to preserving the history of northwestern Arkansas. Several historic buildings from the 19th century, including a log cabin, a doctor's office, and a post office, have been moved to the site. Displays also feature antique photographs, farm equipment, and Native American artifacts.

Prairie Grove Battlefield State Park (Prairie Grove) On December 7, 1862, Confederate and Union forces clashed at this site in a bloody battle. Today, the park features exhibits that bring the world of a Civil War soldier to life. You can also visit a reconstructed 19th-century village.

Buffalo National River (Harrison) Canoeists and rafters love traveling down this river, past towering cliffs and majestic canyons. They can also camp, fish, and hike.

Delta Cultural Center (Helena) At this museum, which is housed in a 1912 train depot, you can learn everything about the Delta, from the roots of the Delta blues to how frequent flooding devastated pioneer farmers.

FUN FACTS

The city of Texarkana straddles the Arkansas-Texas border. It has two city governments, one for each side, but the post office sits exactly on the state line. The building is constructed of half Texas granite and half Arkansas limestone. Its address is Texarkana, Arkansas-Texas.

The only diamond mine in North America is near Murfreesboro, Arkansas. More than 70,000 diamonds have been unearthed since the first was discovered in 1906. The largest found there weighed 40 carats and was named Uncle Sam.

The town of Hector, Arkansas, was named after President Grover Cleveland's dog.

FIND OUT MORE

BOOKS

Beck, Ken and Terry Beck. *President Clinton's Amazing Arkansas: 500 Fabulous Facts.* Nashville, Tenn.: Premium Press America/Spring Creek Books, 1993.

Jameson, W. C. *Buried Treasures of the Ozarks: Legends of Lost Gold, Hidden Silver, and Forgotten Caches.* Little Rock: August House Publishers, 1990.

Young, Richard and Judy Dockery Young. *Ozark Ghost Stories.* Little Rock: August House Publishers, 1995.

VIDEOS

Bear Dog, Bulldog: Talking Traditions and Singing Blues in Arkansas Schools. Co-Media, Inc., 1984. Storytellers and blues musicians in performance at Big Flat and DeVall's Bluff.

I Heard It Through the Grapevine. Talking Traditions, 1984. Fictionalized story about an elementary school student tracking down her family's life stories.

They Tell It for the Truth. Pentacle Productions, Inc., 1981. Performances by some of Arkansas's best tall-tale spinners.

CD-ROM

Story of the States. Parsippany, N.J.: Bureau of Electronic Publishing, CD-ROM available in Macintosh and Windows versions. A multimedia trip to Arkansas and other states of the Union.

INTERNET

www.ardemgaz.com/ Site of Arkansas's largest newspaper, the Little Rock Arkansas Democrat-Gazette.

www.state.ar.us/ Home page for the state of Arkansas.

INDEX

Page numbers for charts, graphs, and illustrations are in boldface.

actors, 92–94, **93**, 133, 135
African Americans, 41,
    44–45, **45**, **80**,
    80–82, **81**, **94**,
    94–96, 128, **128**,
    133, **133**, 134, 135,
    135. *See also* civil
    rights; segregation;
    slavery
agriculture, 17, 38, **43**, **45**,
    59, 61, **62**, **65**,
    79–80, 124
Angelou, Maya, **94**, 94–96,
    127
animals, 24, **25**, 26, 121
    endangered, 122
antiques, 127, 138
archaeology, 136
architecture, **50–51**,
    113–115, 139
Arkansas Post, 33, 34, 123
Arkansas River valley, 16
art, 112, 115, 125. *See also*
    crafts
Ashmore, Harry, 96–98, **97**
Asians, 82
aviation, 112–113, 126

Bates, Daisy, 128, **128**
Bathhouse Row, 115–117
bats, 26
bauxite, 123
Bayou Bartholomew, 16
Beverly Enterprises, 66
birds, 24, 122, 125, 127
    state, 119, **119**
boating, **108**
Boone County, 85
borders, 12, 77, 82, 109,
    117, 121
Bowie, James, 117
Bridges, James, 128

Brock, Lou, 128
bromide, 60
Brown, Dee, 128–129
Brown, Helen Gurley, 129,
    129
Brown, Minnijean, 46
Bryant, Paul "Bear," **129**,
    129–130
businesses, 48–49, 66,
    124, 136

Caldwell, Sarah, 130
Campbell, Glen, 130
canoeing, 138
capital, 119, 123. *See also*
    Little Rock
capitol buildings, **58**,
    113–115, 117
Caraway, Hatty, 123, 130,
    130
Cash, Johnny, 98–99, **99**,
    131
catywhompus, 84–85
Cavelier, René-Robert, 30,
    122
caverns, 109, 137, **137**
celebrations, 41, 61, **73**,
    79, 83, **108**,
    125–127, **126**
chemicals, 60
children, 56–59
Christ of the Ozarks,
    109–112, **112**
cities, 66, **67**
civil rights, 44–48, **46**, **48**,
    96–98, **97**
Civil War, 38–40, **39**, 41,
    117, 123, 127, 138
Cleanup days, 27
Cleveland, Grover, 139
climate, 18–19, 43, 121
Clinton, Bill, 45, 47, 48,

52, 69, 100–103,
    101, **102**, 124, 131
Clinton, Hillary Rodham,
    48, 100
clothing, 77
coal, 60
Conways, 38
courts, **53**, 55–56, 79
crafts, 74, **75**, **111**, 127,
    137
crime, 35, 38, 56, 79, 124
Crockett, Davy, 8, 117
crops, 17, 38, **43**, 61, **62**,
    65, 124, 127
Crowley's Ridge, 17–18, 23
culture, 74–77, 81–83, 89,
    138

dams, 22–23
dance, 74, 125, 126, 127
Dean, Dizzy, 131, **131**
Depression, 43–44, **45**
De Soto, Hernando, 30,
    122
diamonds, 64, 119, 123,
    137, 139
Dodd, David Owen, 40
drought, 43
ducks, 127

eagles, 125
Eckford, Elizabeth, **46**,
    46–47
economy, **57**, 59–69, 124.
    See also poverty
education, 57–59, 72–73,
    123, 131–132
Eisenhower, Dwight D., 47
El Dorado, 42, 123, 128
endangered species, 122,
    122. *See also* wildlife
    refuges

environment, 24–27, **27**, **115**. *See also* wildlife refuges
ethnicity, 72, **73**, **74**, 82–83, 125
Eureka Springs, 126, 137
explorers, 30, 33, 122

Fayetteville, **67**, 123, 126, 130
fish, 24, **63**, 122
floods, 42–43, 138
flowers, **23**, 23–24, 121, **122**, 125
    state, 119, **119**
food, 61, **63**, 74–77, **76**, **78**, 125
Fort Smith, **67**, 79, **79**, 113–115, **114**, 138
frontier spirit, 77–79, **79**. *See also* rodeos
Fulbright, J. William, 131–132, **132**

gas, 60, **65**
geography, 12–18, 121. *See also* lakes; rivers
ghost train, 85
Gilchrist, Ellen, 132
government, 52–56, **53**
governors, 45, 52–54, 73, 97, 100–101, 124
gravel, **65**
Greeks, 125
Green, Al, 132
Green, Ernest, 45–47, **48**
Grisham, John, 132
Gulf Coastal Plain, 16, 59

Helena, **81**, 81–82, 106, 123, 138
highlands, 12–16, **14**, 18, 74–77. *See also* Oachita Mountains; Ozarks
history, 30, 32–41, 77–79, 122–124
hollows, 15–16
Hope, 125, 126, 131
Hot Springs, **67**, 115–117, 129, 131, 133, 137–138

Hot Springs Mountain Tower, 117, 138
Houston, Sam, 117
Huckabee, Mike, 45
Huddleston, John, 64
human services, 56–57
humor, 9

industry, 49, 59–69, **65**, 82, 124

jobs, 52, **65**, 66–67, 79–80
Johnson, John H., 133, **133**
Johnsons, 38
Joplin, Scott, 133

King Biscuit, 82, 126–127
knobs, 16

Ladd, Alan, 133
lakes, **22**, 22–23, 27, **104**, **105**, **108**, 121
landscape, 12–18, **13**, **68**
Latinos, 82–83
legends, 32, 83–86
legislature, 24, 55, 86, 123
Liberty Bell Pavilion, 115
libraries, 123
Little Rock, 34, 35, 45–48, **46**, **48**, **50**, **51**, 57, **58**, **66**, **67**, 113–114, 123, 125, 133
Little Rock Air Force Base, 126
Little Rock Nine, 45–48, **48**
livestock, 59, **62**, **65**, 124. *See also* poultry
Louisiana territory, 30, 122, 123
lowlands, 16–18. *See also* Gulf Coastal Plain; Mississippi Delta
lumber, 59–60, **65**

MacArthur, Douglas, **133**, 133–134
Magazine Mountain, 16
magazines, **34**, 34–35, 129, 133
manufacturing, 124
maps, **2**, **13**, **65**, **107**

McClellan-Kerr Arkansas River System, 124
minerals, 60, 123
Mississippi Delta, 16–18, **17**, 59, 61, 67–69, 79–82, **80**, 106, 138
molasses, 77, **78**
monsters, 83–86
Montana, Patsy, 134, **134**
Mothershed, Thelma, 46–47
motto, 119
Mountain Village 1890, 109, **110**
movies, 92–94, **93**, 113, 128, 132, 133, 134–135
"mudbugs," 24, **25**
Murfreesboro, 64, 123
museums, **78**, 106, 109, **111**, 112–113, **114**, 115–117, 136, 137, 138
music, 74, **75**, 77, **81**, 81–82, 106, 109, 112, 125, 126–127, 138
musicians, 130, 133, 135

name
    of Ozarks, 14
    of state, 12, 34–35, 36–37, 119
Native Americans, 30–32, **31**, 122, 128–129, 136, 138
natural resources, 60, **65**, 117, 123, 124
newspapers, 34–35, 96–98
North Little Rock, 57, **67**
nursing homes, 66

Oachita Mountains, 12, 20–22, 115–117, **116**
observation points, 109, **110–111**, 117, 138
oil, 42, **44**, 59–60, 117, 123
Ozarks, 12–16, **14**, **15**, **19**, 20, 61, 74–77, **78**, 84–85, 109–113, **110**, **111**, 126

paper products, **65**
Parker, Isaac, 79, 113, **114**, 138
parks, **64**, 86, **87**, **115**, 127, 136, 137
Patillo, Melba (Beals), 45–47
pickles, **63**
Pippen, Scottie, 90–92, **91**, 134
plants, 121
    endangered, 122, **122**
poets, **94**, 94–96
politics, 38, 53, 102–103. *See also* governors; senators
population, 33, 35, 38, 42, **42**, **67**
poultry, 49, 59, **65**, 82
poverty, 43–44, **45**, 59, **60**, 69, 72, 79–80
Prairie Grove Battlefield, 127, 138
publishers, **34**, 34–35, 129, 133
pumpkins, 61, **61**

radio, 82
rafting, **116**, 138
rainfall, 18, 42–43, 121
Ray, Gloria, 46–47
razorback hog, 24
recipe, 76
reconstructed village, 138
Reconstruction, 40–41
recreation, 8–9, 83–86, **84**, **87**
religion, 72–73, 81, 82
Reynolds Corp., 67
rice, 61, 127
rivers, 20, **21**, 42–43, **116**, 121, 124, 138
Roberts, Terrence, 46–47, **48**
Robinson, Brooks, 134–135
Rockefeller, Winthrop, 53–54, **54**, 124

Rockefeller, Winthrop Paul, 54
rodeos, **79**, 126

Sanyo Corp., 69
schools, 57–59
segregation, 41, 44–48, 80
senators, 123, 130, 131–132, **132**
settlers, 32–34, 123
Seviers, 38
shape, 12
sharecroppers, **45**
shellfish, 24, **25**
singers, 98–99, **99**, 130, 131, 132, 134
size, 121
slavery, 38, 40
songs, 36–37, 74, 77, 120
spas, 115–117, 137–138
spinning, **111**
sports, **88**, **89**, 90–92, **91**, 128, **129**, 129–130, 131, **131**, 134–135, 135–136. *See also* water sports
springs, 20–22, 115–117, 137–138
statehood, 33, 35, 119, 123
statue, 109–112, **112**
Steele, Frederick, 40
Steenburgen, Mary, 92–94, **93**, 134–135
Still, William Grant, 135, **135**
storytelling, 8–9, 83–86, **84**
Switzer, Barry, 135–136

tall tales, 83–86
Texarkana, 117, 133, 139
textiles, 60
theater, 112, 125
Thomas, Jefferson, 46–47
tomatoes, 125
Tonti, Henri de, 32–33, **33**
Top o' the Ozarks Tower, 109

tornadoes, 18–19
tourism, 49, **68**, 69, 106–117, **107**, 136–138
train, ghost, 85
trees, **23**, 23–24, 59–60, 121
state, 119
Trowbridge, Samuel G., 35
Tucker, Jim Guy, 124
Tyson Foods, 49, 59

University of Arkansas, 24, 123

values, 72, 87
Van Buren, 83, 113
Vietnam memorial, 115

Walker, John H., 12
Walls, Carlotta (LaNier), 46–47, **48**
Wal-Mart, 49, 136
Walton, Sam, 69, 112, 136
Walton Arts Center, 112
Washington, 117
waterfalls, **21**, **28**, **29**
watermelon, 126
water sports, **108**, **116**, 138
websites, 56–57
western region, 77–79, 113–115
White, Frank, 72–73
White River monster, 85–86
white-water rafting, **116**
wildlife refuges, **17**, 137
women, **46**, 46–47, 92–94, **93**, **94**, 94–96, 123, 128, **128**, 129, **129**, 130, **130**, 132
Woodruff, William E., **34**, 34–35, 38
World War II, 44–45
writers, **94**, 94–96; 96–98, **97**, 128–129, 129, **129**, 132